Grief UNVEILED

Advance Praise

Grief Unveiled ever so gently, yet powerfully guides you through the life-changing journey of grief in widowhood. Sarah illustrates the challenges encountered on the path through grief with such tender accessibility, offering both inspiration, empowerment, and solidarity to fellow widows. This is the book for any widow who is ready to move forward in life after loss and thrive.

—**Christina Rasmussen**, author of
Second Firsts: Live, Laugh and Love Again

This book is not merely words on pages and it is not an instructional guide to feeling better in the midst of unspeakable grief. What it is: sacred honesty and gritty hope given alongside companionship; a soft place to land for bruised and weary hearts. Sarah wrote: "feeling to heal is the way out of the quagmire of suffering" and with that one sentence I pressed pause on everything else just to meditate on that wisdom. Her words on intentional grieving and making space for remembering gave me permission to become quiet and not to fear that emptiness. Sarah walks ahead and beside, sharing holy water with us that are so thirsty.

—**Joy Prouty**, portrait artist, Wildflowers Photography

I remember not being able to hold back tears the first time I heard Sarah's story. Partly because of what she experienced, but more so because I was overwhelmed by the amount of beauty, joy, love and vibrance surrounding her, reflected in her friends and family. With this book, her words, her story and her wisdom can help you do the same. What a gift.

—**Elizabeth DiAlto**, host of the Untame the Wild Soul
Podcast, author of *Untame Yourself*

Author Sarah M. Nannen is a masterful and eloquent wordsmith. In Grief Unveiled she uses her gift to translate the unspeakable emotions of loss while introducing a beacon of light where there was only darkness. The book outlines wisdom and guidance on how to reclaim one's life after sudden tragedy offering genuine hope for a new tomorrow. Read and re-read Grief Unveiled… then share it with others!

—**Patti Smith**, President of America's Gold Star Families

Grief
UNVEILED

A Widow's Guide to Navigating
Your Journey in Life After Loss

SARAH NANNEN

NEW YORK

LONDON • NASHVILLE • MELBOURNE • VANCOUVER

Grief UNVEILED

A Widow's Guide to Navigating Your Journey in Life After Loss

Published in New York, New York, by Morgan James Publishing in partnership with Difference Press. Morgan James is a trademark of Morgan James, LLC. www.MorganJamesPublishing.com

The Morgan James Speakers Group can bring authors to your live event. For more information or to book an event visit The Morgan James Speakers Group at www.TheMorganJamesSpeakersGroup.com.

ISBN 978-1-68350-750-5 paperback
ISBN 978-1-68350-751-2 eBook
Library of Congress Control Number: 2017913739

Cover Design by:
Rachel Lopez
www.r2cdesign.com

Interior Design by:
Bonnie Bushman
The Whole Caboodle Graphic Design

In an effort to support local communities, raise awareness and funds, Morgan James Publishing donates a percentage of all book sales for the life of each book to Habitat for Humanity Peninsula and Greater Williamsburg.

Get involved today! Visit
www.MorganJamesBuilds.com

For the feather sisters that helped me see my wings.

Table of Contents

Note From The Author

In this book, you'll read words written to and about widows burying their husbands. Our language and cultural views are limited around grief, just as they are around partnering, gender identity, and the infinitely magical ways we love. I've used feminine gendered words for ease of communication and I'm asking you to hear whatever language is applicable to however you identified inside your love story and whoever you loved. This book is for widows burying their beloveds. It's for all the broken hearts who deeply loved their someone who died. Regardless of your title, identity, status, or timeline, no one can take your love or your grief from you. Your grief is allowed. Your love is deep and true. Even in death, love is love.

There will be moments that my thoughts and ideas will challenge your beliefs and perhaps deeply trigger you in an unexpected way. Instead of rejecting what elicits a powerful response in you, I invite you to take a deep breath and give yourself the opportunity to move through what you've read. The path toward healing often begins in the trigger. Go gently into the pages of this book. Take small bites. Give yourself time to reflect before moving on. Let the concepts roll around in your head and heart. Let it be food for thought. Take along only what works for you, for now. Circle back when it feels right to digest again.

Introduction

This is a love letter whispered from a wife turned widow. I'm writing from a future life after loss I didn't used to believe in; a postcard from possibility. I see you there with the hollow look in your eyes. You're aching deep inside as you scrape together the remnants of a beautiful life lost when he died. The world around you feels superficial now. Where once there was love and dreams, there is ache and emptiness. There is a very felt sense of duty in grieving and you don't want to get it wrong. Your pain provides the only felt connection to him that remains. Any fleeting moment of joy gets rejected as less real than the all-encompassing longing. You want to believe in hope and a better someday but you can't even bring yourself to dream. Joy tastes like guilt and betrayal now, anyway.

I see you there with days blurring together, some lasting an eternity. Time doesn't make sense with everything filtered through this sadness. Nothing really makes sense, if you're honest. Most days, you're numb, going through the motions until you can collapse in the nighttime privacy of tears and exhaustion. Some days you barely remember. Some days you can't muster the strength to even begin. People ask you about your future and what you'll do without him. They *want* you to know. What they can't know is how incapacitated you feel when it comes to knowing anything at all. You're barely able to wrap your mind around what's happening tomorrow, maybe even later today, let alone whether or not you'll move or go back to work. Anything feels like too much to know.

I see you there inside the trepidation, wondering how you could ever *want* to carry on, if it's truly even possible. The aching brokenness and yearning feels so permanent. The best you can imagine for your life is surviving this. That seems to be all anyone expects of you now anyway: don't get *too* sad, don't screw your kids up *too* bad, put your head down, push through and keep his memory alive. The day he died, it's as though your new life's mission was assigned and there was no honorable option to decline. Somewhere deep inside, you've already decided any life you might manage to reclaim after this loss will always pale in comparison.

I see you there wondering if you're doing it right. *Are my choices making it all worse? Am I healthy? Is this safe? Am I crying too much? Should I be crying more? Should I be feeling better by now? How do I know if I'm depressed…or worse?* I see you inside these swirling thoughts of panic, desperate to be ok. I know what it's like to be desperate to get your grief right.

I'm here to whisper to you until you know it's true in your soul: this is normal, you can't get it wrong, you don't require fixing, and you're not alone. Your pain is real and important. Your suffering doesn't have to be forever. This love letter is not about measuring your grief against a proper metric. This book isn't written with step-by-step instructions for how to get better. It's simply to create a safe space for you to be seen, held, and heard. It's about learning how to feel so you can begin to heal.

I see you there inside the invisibility of grief. Everyone is watching your life after loss but so few can actually see the reality of what that means. When faced with aloneness in grief, we do everything we can to protect the people remaining in our world. You dry your tears before anyone can see. The words *I'm OK* come spilling out of your mouth in a hurried lie you're hoping one day will feel true. You show up, push through, and press on to assure your people, and perhaps yourself too, that you really are OK. You keep *trying* to be OK, whispering prayers that one day this pain will go away.

The unspoken rules of what it means to be a widow feel etched in stone, and reality too. *What do I want? What is allowed? What do I need? What is real? Is this clarity or is this just crazy?* Searching for answers that feel true inside your grief is like grasping for a lifeline from inside the sinking quicksand. You're never sure what's safe to hold onto. You're trying so hard to get it right. Behind every decision you face, there's doubt and second-guessing yourself.

I still recall my own depletion, overwhelm and hopelessness in grief. I can remember the constant longing for someone to save me from this nightmare, always lingering just under my skin. I didn't want to hear about hope for a happy life after loss. All I wanted was him. All I wanted was for none of it to be real. You don't need silver linings. You can't tolerate one more explanation of God's will and his "perfect" timing. Even when you very much believe in God, having his death explained away feels like salt in a wound.

I'm not doing any of that here. None of this is about forgetting or bypassing pain for a pretend happiness. Grieving with support and intention is your lifeline. Feeling to heal is the way out of the quagmire of suffering. This book is an invitation to explore a less traveled path through grief that makes the way forward feel more yours for the taking.

This work is not about letting go. It's about encountering your authentic Self within your grief, and as a result, accessing true healing. We're inviting in healing to ease the suffering. We're inviting in living to replace the surviving. We're creating space for remembering and feeling that one day becomes wholeness and thriving.

You and only you will be the heroine of your story. You cannot wish hard enough to bring him back. You cannot cry adequate tears to make any of this untrue. There is no going back. There is no one to save you. But, there is you, and I'm here to tell you this one thing: *you are enough.* You have everything you need to begin. You are in exactly the right place, with courage enough to open this book. You don't have to do it alone. You don't even have to believe in it yet to begin. You've come to this place because you're open to the possibility of something more than surviving in life after loss. The rest of your life is yours and it's waiting. Let's begin.

Chapter One

A Journey Into Grief

I felt the cruel reality of widowhood slam into place when I saw the Marine Corps officers in full dress uniform standing on my porch. *No. Please! Not him. Not me. This can't be real. Not this. Anything but this.*

I wondered as I missed him so desperately inside every moment: *Is this really all my life will ever be now—sadness, longing, and despair? Will I ever wake up feeling alive again? Will my heart ever truly sing without the accompaniment of grief's sting? Won't any ray of happiness always just be second best to this story I've lost?*

We each have our own perceptions of what life after loss will look like. Within our lived stories of grief, we find the truth of our experiences to be vastly different than the way society has painted it to be. While the journey will be different for each of us, it's important to understand grief is a passage to be actively navigated. Grief is not a lifetime sentence; it's a hard road to be traveled. It's not something to suffer; it's something to move through. Without a bird's eye view of grief, it's hard to find your footing on the rocky terrain or even see the path ahead. Let's take a look at the topography of this path you never wanted to walk, yet lies before you all the same.

BECOMING THE WIDOW

One day you were living with your beloved by your side: paying bills, making plans, and loving life. For better or worse, in sickness and in health, he was yours and life was good. Like a switch on the tracks, his death violently and immediately twisted the course of your life in a direction you'd never choose. A devastating and terminal diagnosis. An instantaneous tragedy no one saw coming. All horrific. All traumatic. All too soon. All of it now part of your story. Time and function all froze when you heard them say it, nothing but the slow pulse of heartbeat and ringing in your ears. It all felt impossible. That he was dead. That you were now a widow. That you were left here to do it alone.

Almost immediately, people were asking you to show up. There were papers to sign. There were decisions to be made. There were bills to be paid. People needed to hug you. People needed you to hug them. But mostly, people needed you to *somehow* be OK. You didn't want this. You don't want any of this. You want the life you were living before he was dead; the life you were living together. The fog of grief is relentless. There's a felt sense of slowly losing yourself in it. You're exhausted. You're moving between the agony of longing and absolute numbness. You feel life as you know it coming unraveled. You're just trying to make it through each day. Life is about surviving now. It all feels more like being swallowed whole by the pain than living.

YOUR STOLEN SOMEDAY

Your life was so full before he died; always on the move, always working hard. You were living for your someday. *Someday there will be more time together. Someday life will be easier. Someday we'll look back and know this hard work was just the beautiful path to bring us here together.* There's no someday to steer toward now, not one you'd ever want anyway. You find yourself paddling frantically away from pain whenever possible, but never sure where you're heading. The truth is, so often you simply let go and submerge into the depths of pain because he somehow feels closer at hand there. Nothing makes sense in that space, but somehow everything does too. And so, you sink roots down deep into the pain of grief where you know how to love him still.

WHEN GRIEF FEELS LIKE LOVE

The word *widow* feels so hopelessly small, but you cling to the comfort of that identity anyway. It feels like the one tangible piece of loving him you have left. To be his widow allows you claim to continue loving him beyond the grave. That word gives you someone to be without him by your side. Your life after loss has become dedicated to remembering your beloved and the story you shared.

There is urgency behind the remembering; proving over and over to your broken open heart that it ever really happened at all. With each tear, you whisper back to life what's been lost, if only for a moment. Your sadness feels like the only tangible expression of how much you love him and you never, ever want to lose that. You feel the enormity of this task and dedicate yourself wholly to it. Your new title is universally understood to be a lifetime's work. You've now got a job to do. You're his widow: the keeper of his memory.

HOW LONG IS FOREVER?

They tell us grief is enormous. They say it lasts forever. They tell you that's normal and that's OK. Time marches on, oblivious to the depth of grief ripping through your reality. You are asked to begin again day after day, to face this storm and stay the weary, wandering, fog-filled course toward something called living that feels so foreign right now it seems impossible to be moving toward anything at all.

Time heals all, they tell you. And so, you wait for forever to be over. You wait out your grief. But from your knees, forever does not seem long enough to heal this hurt. The suffering remains. And then one day, you find yourself graveside, wondering if any of it was ever real. You see his name etched in stone and even after all the decisions, longing, and tears, it's still surreal to see his name spelled out there with such finality. This is the moment the journey into grief becomes real and you find yourself searching for where to begin.

GRIEF: THE VILLAIN

Grief is often misunderstood as being a cruel and heartless human experience we're forced to endure. We see those in mourning as victims of tragedy instead of people living out the inevitable reality of mankind. However intense and painful the grief experience may be, what's actually happening in the meticulous, irreplaceable process of grief is a systematic rewiring of our personal reality. It's triggered by the deeply felt loss of someone that was intrinsic to our sense of Self and it hurts deeply. The ground shifts out from under you when it strikes, leaving you grasping for anything solid to hold onto.

Humanity has always tried to explain the unexplainable. Inherent to the cultural systems we've created to do just that are the stories to explain and manage our most primal and deeply felt human experiences. We're all guaranteed to experience grief at some point in life. As a result, there is a culturally rich history of stories cautioning against what becomes of us when someone we love dies. And so, we come to the modern day iteration of belief systems surrounding grief, guided by the deeply embedded, proper Puritan roots of Western culture and painted colors of Hollywood "reality".

We have created the most impossible of dichotomies in grief between what we think is expected and what we actually experience. As a result, we harshly judge our lived experience against these stories and suffer all the more deeply. Combined with the sensed judgment of the people around us bad as the grief. You want to live again but you don't want to do it without him.

WHAT WILL BECOME OF ME?

In my new role as widow, it seemed like I had been replaced by the fatal disease of mourning that might be contagious and was certainly fragile. In my earliest dance with grief, everyone I encountered treated me with great caution. Years later, some still do. Those with the courage to come toward my pain felt they didn't know what to say to me. Often, they said nothing. Some apologized for crying beside me. No one knew how to be with me because no one knew how to save me. They thought that's what I needed them to do. They saw only my story of loss, equally fascinating and horrifying. I was now a thing to be pitied with no hope for healing.

I'm here to stand beside you inside that swirling storm others aren't sure how to weather with you. I see you. I know you don't need saving. I believe in your someday even if you aren't ready to yet. As the sun rises each day, your story of life after loss is being written. I know this road feels too much to bear. I see you there in it because I have been on my knees on that same dot on that same forsaken map. I want you to know this task before you to stay the course of living doesn't mean what you think.

I, too, once misunderstood my charge as a widow, calling on strength to power my way through with only self-preservation and determination as refuge and guide. I refused to become the stereotype, determined to do grief *right*. For so long, I refused to come undone, and did everything I could to avoid feeling the depth of my own pain. I, too, once turned to pushing through the pain, trying my best to go back to living. I learn that when you bypass the wild darkness of your pain, you're left with nothing but mangled remnants of Self trailing behind you. When, instead, you point yourself in the direction of moving with and through the ache of grief, you slowly find your way home to your Self and a life that feels true and whole too. This is the journey through grief.

THE NECESSITY OF GRIEF

You honor his memory not with forever longing but with intentional grief. Sadly, we rarely have a model for what that might look like. In Western cultures and perhaps more and more worldwide, we've sterilized, internalized, and privatized our grief to the point that so few of us have seen our elders or peers express deep, primal, painful emotion or the ritual of remembrance. So often, we rarely even see one another truly weep. We have no felt permission to deeply grieve nor a map to follow into the shadowland that is mourning. We simply attempt to survive it. We keep it tidy and quiet. We're called things like *inspiring* and *strong* when we do. We keep our pain a big secret locked away inside for only the most private moments of release. In doing so, we miss the deeply profound experience that is fundamental to the processing our psyche requires to initiate healing.

We've been told mourning comes at us in five stages. It paints a picture of grief that is tidy, organized, and run by a rigid structure of rules it will follow. The stories say if we can just hold on tight enough and long enough, we'll manage to survive. We literally believe we can outlast grief, waiting until it fades away. We power through. We *try*. And we continue to ache, our broken hearts literally rotting away inside our bellies, left unattended to in the name of being OK.

Somewhere throughout the ages, we've lost our ability to honor the necessity of mourning and its vital role in the "psychic immune system," of our humanness, as Marianne Williamson put it. I'm writing because along my journey through grief, I found another path no one told me about. This path felt safe to take but was definitely not easy. You see, there is another model of grief in the aftermath of tragic loss that facilitates deep and powerful healing. So few know about it and even fewer are talking about it. This journey through grief brings you to a place of healing that is capable of powerfully transforming who you are and the way you live. It's a path I've walked and one I know others have found their way onto. It's yours to travel too, should you choose it. It's for anyone willing to lean into the journey and all they'll encounter there.

They say grief lasts forever. I say, grief leaves you forever changed but that does not have to mean forever suffering. Grief is an intense, hard-wired response of mind, body, and spirit to the death of someone we love. Its entire purpose is to facilitate healing so we may process, evolve and step into life again. When we grieve with intention instead of bracing against it or waiting it out, we allow ourselves to come fully undone and fully human. We methodically process the death and our new reality. We intentionally tend to our gaping hearts and troubled minds. Along the way, we learn to live in the present. In doing so, we come to understand how to keep the beautiful memories of what has been without the pain.

INVITING TRANSFORMATION

Grief and the death that screamed it to life are companions, yet very separate entities. His death is forever but your journey into grief is not guaranteed to swallow you whole, as the stories tell us. Artist Man Andrews said of grief, "it becomes something you can hold rather than something that overwhelms you—a part of you rather than a burden." When we get powerful enough to create space to grieve instead of pushing it away, a subtle shift takes place. Instead of protecting ourselves from grief, we curate permission to let it be. We move through this shadowland toward hope, healing and transformation. It's not a silver lining of grief; it's the whole point. Even with the heartbreak it brings to your story, grief is also draping your heavy shoulders with a cloak of transformation. You won't be able to see it for some time, perhaps, but it's there and it's happening. Everyone thinks they know exactly what life after loss looks like. I certainly thought I knew. I'm so glad I was wrong.

REFLECTION

We often believe grief has to look a certain way, especially as a widow. These beliefs can be so fixed as truth in our minds that they challenge our actual experiences. Take a moment right now to think about what you believe your widowhood means to you and even perhaps what it means *about* you. Consider which beliefs you've inherited from cultural stories and which are informed by your lived experiences. To understand where to begin your journey into grief, you must bring your beliefs into your full awareness. Free write what feels most true for you right now as you complete the prompts below:

- *As a widow, what I feel most afraid of is…*
- *As a widow, what I feel most limited by is…*
- *As a widow, what I wish other people understood is…*
- *As a widow, what I am most surprised by is…*
- *As a widow, I am ready to…*

Chapter Two

The Chrysalis

I wish to stop time for you to step outside the onslaught of life that swirls on all around you, oblivious to your pain. A million people need you to make ten million decisions, and a thousand more want simply to tell you they care. What I really want to offer you is a quiet and a safe space to collapse for a little while. I'd love to give you time to reflect, remember, and fold inward to feel safe in the surreal and numbing comfort of being fully engulfed by the heartbreak for a while.

I want to hand you permission to let go of the hustle and find a place where you can relax into a heap. No questions to answer. No decisions to make. Nothing you're supposed to have figured out. No task to tend to. No dinner to make. Simply space to dive under the murky waters and just *be* for a while, letting the river of grief and memories wash over the jagged pit of your pain. That's all we ever want on our darkest days: to be seen in an authentic way from deep within the safety of solitude and space to just be. This space to soften and come undone is where we begin our journey into grief.

THE CHRYSALIS

During my training with Martha Beck, I was blown away by her use of the life cycle of a butterfly as a metaphor for transformation resulting from struggle. The chrysalis holds space for the fragile, confusing, magic of metamorphosis within. In the chrysalis, you're neither a caterpillar nor a butterfly. Without the chrysalis, there is no becoming. The stillness is where the healing happens. Without it, you stay in the pain, stuck in the exhausting dance of outlasting your grief. It's the place you'll come back to over and over throughout the remainder of your journey through grief; the refuge you'll revisit after every summit and storm. The chrysalis is the key to finding your way through to your life after loss on the other side.

SAFE HAVEN FOR HEALING

Despite the incredible pain, the death of your beloved has initiated the process of metamorphosis-of-Self and there's no stopping it now. Like the caterpillar changing physical states, everything you know is coming undone in the aftermath of his death. Just as the caterpillar creates a safe place to come completely unraveled, we must do so too in the depth of our pain. When the caterpillar senses her unraveling is imminent, she meticulously begins creating a protected place for the intense and extremely vulnerable process of metamorphosis to occur. Creating a silk pad on the underside of a branch to attach upside-down to, she then literally comes undone, shedding her skin to reveal the chrysalis. She's in a most vulnerable state and requires absolute stillness now to make it through to the other side. Safely inside where no one can see, the now skinless caterpillar transforms into a liquidish mass of cells that will one day become a butterfly. Her work isn't done, but she's safe to undertake the slow process of becoming within the chrysalis.

HOW WILL I KNOW WHEN?

During the journey through grief, it's easy to identify with that formless, skinless, goo that was once a fuzzy caterpillar. Nothing makes sense. Everything is too loud, too fast, too much, and too soon. This overwhelm is telling you it's time to create the chrysalis. It's time to slow down and turn inward. It's time to stop running from it and make space for everything that is aching within you and changing around you.

When you force away the stillness you so deeply need, you relegate yourself to existing as post-caterpillar goo without a chrysalis and little to no hope of attaining butterfly status no matter how hard you work at it. In grief, making space for stillness and a pace of life you can manage is essential to your healing.

There will still be days you'll want desperately to go back to being a caterpillar, longing for the life you knew before he died. You've been wearing yourself weary to the bone, trying to go back to a "normal" life. You've been pushing and striving and strong-arming your way toward something that no longer exists. When you find yourself aching inside a life you don't recognize as yours, it's time to make space for the transformation. The metamorphosis cannot happen without the chrysalis.

TAKE BACK THE PACE

To begin constructing your chrysalis, your first task is to slow down enough for your pain to come through. When faced with trauma, crisis, and the agony of heartbreak, our bodies physically respond by preparing for action to escape. Slowing down to experience the pain is the *last* thing on our mind when grief strikes. Our survival center tells us to reject it all, resist and run. So, we do. We run hard and we run fast. Once we notice ourselves attempting to outrun our pain, we realize how exhausted we are. We notice not only our exhaustion, but our anxiety, fear, and self-doubt too. There's a no tolerance policy for these experiences in the chrysalis. Within the chrysalis, we're curating a life of peace, empowerment, and knowing.

EXHAUSTION

When exhausted enough, you become numb to feeling. Because you're so aware of the acute discomfort of your physical body's sheer depletion, there's no energy left to investigate the ache of your heart and soul. You operate purely in survival mode. Life is about getting through the day. The notion of self-care is altogether abandoned in your survival state. As your physical depletion increases, your emotional ache is felt all the more deeply. You're trying so hard and until you stop *trying*, you'll never feel better.

The healing you'll experience on your journey through grief must begin in your physical body, meeting your own most basic needs. We humans are wired for survival, and physical healing precedes matters of head and heart, every time. Until you create a pace of life committed to adequate sleep, calm, safety, and nourishment, you remain in an activated survival response. Your thoughts and emotions are essentially fixed and inaccessible there. By creating the chrysalis, you commit to a life that supports physical health and safety at its roots to facilitate deeper healing of heart and soul, too.

ON FATIGUE AND DEPRESSION

Anyone who's experienced grief knows exhaustion is part of the territory. Most also know that fatigue can be an indicator of depression and many even associate grief with depression interchangeably. It's important to make the distinction and learn to use discernment when meeting your own needs in grief. Raise your hand if you've in the middle of the night asked Google: "is this grief or depression?" What's asked of you in grief is endless, and when you experience exhaustion, it's easy to panic. *It's not safe to lay in bed and stare at the wall for an entire day,* we tell ourselves.

THE RIGHT TO REST

The sheer enormity of bearing heartbreak while tending to the endless to-do lists that go with burying your beloved requires Herculean strength. Rachael was exhausted to the bone. She ached physically and she ached emotionally, too. She told me she wanted nothing more than to spend an entire day in bed. *It's all I can think about,* she said. *I want to just have an entire day to climb into the comfort of my covers and stay there.* When asked why she hadn't done it since her husband died eight months earlier, she told me very pointedly *because you know…depression. It's not safe. Right?* Rachael was abandoning her deepest felt needs from a place of fear.

When we ignore our needs, we experience suffering which is actually more likely to lead to depression than a single, longed-for day spent in the comfort of bed. There's a difference between choosing rest because you need it and being incapacitated to the point that getting out of bed doesn't occur to you as a viable option. There's such relief that comes from allowing your exhaustion to be real without making it pathological. There's a time to ask for support if depression rears it's head, but please consider the possibility that choosing to slow down, feel, and require more rest to manage your journey does not always mean you are depressed. Exhaustion is fundamental to grief and our fear of slowing down actually perpetuates it, prolonging our felt pain. In tending to our needs for rest, support, and comfort in grief, we're creating a state for healing. This is the chrysalis.

DEMANDING STILLNESS

Find stillness. Demand it if you must. Hire help for a time if that's what it takes. Let your shoulders relax and your breath slow down. This stillness allows your physiology to relax too; no survival response needed. Your blood pressure slows. Your heart rate slows. No longer on the run, you remember what it is to be at rest. You feel your feet touch the ground, melting away the urgency to escape. The pain does not recede immediately, but the anxiety is slowly released. Healing is initiated in the stillness. Slowly, slowly, slowly. This is the chrysalis.

BLUEPRINT FOR THE CHRYSALIS

There is no one way to build and maintain a metaphorical chrysalis in life after loss. Building a chrysalis to navigate your grief from within isn't about taking a nap twice a week, although it's a start. It's taking an overhead look at every piece of your life and noticing where you're experiencing frenzy, chaos and panic to replace it with stillness, peace, and ease.

BUT I'M TOO BUSY

During our work together, Lisa came to realize the lived importance of the chrysalis. Like so many others, she was depleted and frustrated that nothing she did helped lift her anxiety or exhaustion. We began by looking at her day-to-day life. After taking in the reality of her current daily life, we zoomed out to look at the upcoming month and then the next three months.

I asked her a lot of questions about the things on her schedule and to-do list. With few exceptions, everything she was putting her energy into were things she felt like she *should* do. Most of them she felt like she *had to do*. These were the same pieces of her life where she felt most weary and anxious. *Most of my day feels like life is slowly being sucked out of me. I'm constantly doing all these things that I'm supposed to do to feel better, but I just feel more tired. I'm always scheduling appointments and connecting with friends and it all feels so empty. I hate how small my life is now, and how exhausted I constantly feel too. I feel like I'm sleep-walking my way through someone else's life,* she told me.

We systematically worked through her life, day by day at first, and explored every single thing she was committing time and energy to. It took some serious time and in-depth support to get really clear on the *why* behind each of her current choices to understand what her chrysalis realistically could look like. Lisa immediately heard a borage of thoughts telling her why her life was going to have to be hard and exhausting. *Maybe everyone else can have a chrysalis, but not me,* she kept saying. Instead of becoming enslaved by her limiting beliefs around what she thought was impossible, Lisa got intentional about looking at the life she was allowing in. She got serious about letting go of the things that were unnecessary, things she didn't want in the first place, and particularly those items that created anxiety and exhaustion. Months later with her chrysalis fully in place, and continuing to carefully cultivate her days by choosing what did and did not get time and energy in her chrysalis, Lisa told me she finally felt like she was truly living *her* life.

Lisa worked hard to get really clear about the concept of choice in her life. We all have it, yet we each continue to suffer, forgetting over and over that everything we do is a choice. Even if it doesn't feel like it, there is always choice. Sure everything comes with consequences, good and bad, but we always have the power to choose. When we choose intentionally, we wind up living a life much more aligned with our true needs and desires. This creates space for metamorphosis. This is the chrysalis.

FINDING YOUR BALANCE

This process takes time and putting it into practice is a constantly moving target. Think about tightrope walkers carrying the long stick horizontally in front of them for balance. They're slowly placing their feet, constantly shifting their weight left and right, sometimes stepping back to readjust their weight distribution and the tension on the line below them. This is what we do with all this healing work we're brewing. We constantly adjust for balance in the present moment, not for what's *right* but instead for what we most need. We slow down enough to feel what's there. We curate enough stillness in our days to actually feel what's happening below the surface of our busy-ness. We create space to feel so we may heal.

YOU DON'T NEED TO BE FIXED

There's just one more thing we need to make clear before going any further. You've likely come here with the belief that from inside your grief, you need to be either fixed or saved. Neither is true. You're embarked on a journey you never set out to do. You're grieving, which is a human experience that happens way down deep inside what we call *shadow*. It's the dark, scary, primal experience you spent a lot of energy keeping at bay before bringing your chrysalis into being. It makes you panic and feel anxious. It makes you feel unseen and sometimes insane. You're in a real place full of real pain, but you certainly don't need to be saved. It's a profound experience you're moving through. You're on your way.

We're going to get to work in the chapters to come, for sure. But we're not fixing and we're not saving, unless you're ready to call *yourself* the heroine of this story. We're excavating. We're digging up everything that's buried inside you to be slowly brought into the light. There's no fixing to be done, but you're sure as hell walking the powerful journey to release, reclaim, and heal.

OWNING YOUR KNOWING

You're going to want me or someone to simply tell you what to do to get better. You'll want someone else to know how to face your pain and provide the emergency CPR to bring you fully back to life and yourself again. I can hear rushing up from your belly the question: *Yes, but how will I KNOW? How will I know what's right and what's wrong? How will I know what's real and what I need? How will I know what's healthy and what's a spiral toward depression or worse? How will I know?* I know you're asking these questions because they're the same ones we all ask inside these deep dark shadow moments of grief, pain, and transformation as we build the chrysalis.

It will always, always come back to this: only you can ever know *and* choose what it is you most deeply need. Others can help you find your way there, but you've got to invite them in. Even then, only you can choose. Only you can act. Only you can show up for the journey. They'll help you lean in to ask the questions, and hold you accountable to waiting for the response that comes not from your head, but from deep down in your belly. That answer is always true and always from You.

REFLECTION

Knowing the chrysalis is about stillness and ease, can you see any of that in your day-to-day life currently? Spend some time examining the responsibilities and activities in your life and consider what you might safely eliminate, reschedule, or ask for help with. Notice when your head immediately takes over and tells you it *has* to be the way it is. Instead of worrying about how you might implement a change or dismissing it as impossible, simply notice what it is that feels like peace, joy, or ease. Free write what feels most true for you right now as you complete the prompts below:

- *I feel most exhausted when…*
- *I feel scared when…*
- *There would be more space for stillness in my life if…*
- *If I could change anything about my life right now (knowing I can't bring anyone back to life), it would be…*
- *To experience stillness, I would have to ask for help with…*
- *To me, ease looks like…*

Chapter Three

The In-Between of Grief

Embarking on the journey into grief does not bring instant clarity and closure. In fact, it plops you smack dab into the in-between of grief where everything is even hazier now that you've stopped trying to dodge the pain. Your senses seem slow to notice and quick to overwhelm. Tears linger close to the surface. Time doesn't exactly make sense. Conversations often seem surreal. Actually, nothing feels quite real. The fog of grief steals pieces of your day and things you were supposed to remember. Smells and songs make you cry. Nothing makes you cry. Everything makes you cry. Sometimes you're too tired to cry. You feel like you're in a bizarre performance for no one that everyone is watching.

You're working hard to get it right and looking for signs that you're going to be OK.

You still haven't figured out how to answer that question that just keeps coming: *How are you?* You wonder the same thing three hundred times a day. *How am I? Am I OK? Is this OK? Am I going over the edge? Is this sickness or is this sadness? Is this grief or is this depression? How do I know how I am?* There seems to be no knowing, there is only doing your best to get it right, at least for today. You're no longer his wife. You're no longer the girl you can barely remember being before you were his wife either, so you hover somewhere in the middle. You're terrified of who this means you must become. As Nancy Levine put it, this is "the space between no longer and not yet." This is the in-between of grief.

ONE STEP FORWARD

It's murky and uncomfortable here in the in-between of grief, as though you're standing alone somewhere in the middle of a long suspension bridge. Looking back at the direction you've come from (your life before he died), it's clear that direction is no longer passable. You can't go back. You've got no idea what lies on the other side or how long it will take to get there. You're so exhausted, the idea of getting there at all seems an impossibility.

The in-between of grief is about taking in everything you've been trying to outrun, outsmart, and outlast. It's about coming fully present, face to face with the reality you've found yourself living, as painful as it may be. The in-between is about claiming your grief without making plans to stay. It's about acknowledging what you find there. Moving through the in-between is where you first begin to take action instead of surviving the painful ride. No longer a passive thing to survive, your grief now becomes intentional. This is not about letting it go, getting over it, or closure. It's simply about claiming the truth of your life as it is right now and learning to notice how you feel.

NOTHING'S WORKING

Fay was one of my earliest clients whose husband died a few years before our first call. She contacted me feeling completely frustrated by grief. *No matter what I do, I just keep feeling horrible. Nothing's working and nothing makes sense. I'm always so stressed and scared. I'm so tired of it all,* she complained to me. She proceeded to tell me all the ways she was doing what she thought were the *right* things to heal. She told me about her strict workout regimen to stave off depression. She told me how she was forcing herself to go for coffee with friends when they called, putting on a happy face so they'd keep inviting her. She talked about how hard she was trying not to cry too much. She even told me despite the fact that she hated her job, she continued going, unwilling to *give in to her pain,* as she put it. She told me she didn't know who she was anymore so she just kept doing what she had always done except none of it felt real now. Fay was in the in-between of grief.

During our work together, Fay learned to observe the facts of her reality instead of doing whatever she thought was right to avoid feeling pain. One of the tools that helped Fay find her footing in the in-between was cultivating an awareness of her thoughts and feelings by simply naming them in a journal.

She would jot down things like: *I am aware that I feel lonely. I am aware that I miss him. I am aware that I feel small and scared. I am aware that I don't want to go tomorrow.* She practiced noticing what was true in her life after loss in terms of "right now," paying special attention to what she was feeling and not immediately forcing it away in exchange for what she *thought* she should feel.

In doing so, Fay was able to start choosing what she most needed instead of forcing herself to choose a life she thought she should want. When Fay stopped assigning meaning to her reality at any given moment and forcing it away, she felt more ease in the unfamiliar territory of the in-between of grief. Instead of strong-arming her way through each day, she was now able to consider carefully how each decision made her feel and listen more closely to the whisper deep within telling her what she needed. She learned to skip anything that feels like forcing and frantic performance. With just this awareness, Fay told me everything about her grief journey felt so much more accessible and safe.

ALLOWING WHAT IS

One of the first steps you take to move through the in-between of grief is to simply notice what you notice. You can make this hard and you might try to for a while, but it's literally the practice of watching your own thoughts. What's hard is learning to observe your thoughts like a passive observer rather than a panel of judges. We spend an exorbitant amount of time and energy trying to judge our way through grief, pushing away anything that feels unsafe, confusing or irrational. We're literally navigating our grief, sizing up every choice, feel, and scenario for potential judgment and additional pain. When we instead just notice what we notice, we become the guru. We observe our thoughts and feelings as data. This is the beginning of intentional grief.

Liberation comes when you no longer need to explain, justify, or run from what it is you experience. We bring our needs, experiences and intuition to the center of our healing and take it as information about how to proceed. "Enlightenment has more to do with embracing reality than escaping it," spiritual teacher Adyashanti tells us. When you notice what you notice, you simply allow *what is* to be. You don't have to ask for permission. You don't make yourself wrong. You don't criticize, judge, or make it mean anything about you or your moral character. You don't run it through the filter of religion or science to make it real. You don't rush to explain it away to protect your understanding of the world, either. You simply allow it to be. Noticing what you notice facilitates ease in the uncomfortable in-between of grief.

THE FOUNDATION OF SELF-CARE

In noticing what you notice, you're practicing the art of being able to meet your own needs. Self-care isn't about a bath and a couple of candles, it's about learning to notice your pain and holding it tenderly so it may move through. When you notice you feel sad, you create space for the sadness. Instead of putting on a happy face and faking it away, you let the tears come and create a comforting and safe space for your sadness that isn't hidden away in your closet at midnight.

When you notice you're completely exhausted, instead of powering through in the name of being OK, you create space for rest and ask for help. You hire help if you have to. When you notice you miss talking to him, instead of making it a ridiculous and impossible thing to want, you find a way to communicate with him that feels safe and true for you, whether in a journal or out loud at a place special to you. You notice yourself longing for his scent just one more time and so you dig out some of his old t-shirts and inhale deeply instead of continuing the agony of longing. When you begin creating space for what you notice, you'll slowly replace panic with peace and anxiety with ease in the in-between of grief.

GRIEF IS AN AND THING

I look back and see myself having a margarita with a dear friend, laughing and sobbing in the same moments just two months after my husband's death. I hadn't seen her in years and it felt so good to be in her safe company; she was interested in my true experience not the projection of *I'm OK*. And yet, within me there was so much guilt and distrust of my capacity to feel joy alongside my devastation in that moment of connection with her. *What kind of widow was I to feel anything other than pain, even if the joy was fleeting?*

That day we joked about not being able to post to social media the smiling selfie we had taken together with margarita glasses hoisted, except we weren't joking. Even with our tear-stained cheeks captured in the shot, I couldn't help but wonder: *what would people think to see me looking happy and so soon?* I thought it was my fear of their judgment that kept me from sharing the picture, but it was actually the judgment I was casting on myself. The juxtaposition of the ache and the joy left me wrestling with my reality. When all the feels came at me together, none of it felt real. In the confusion of the in-between of my grief, I felt like I couldn't even trust my own feelings now. I had only just begun to notice what I noticed.

That I could laugh so hard I cried did not mean I could not also, in the same moment, ache so hard inside I sometimes wanted to die. This can be incredibly confusing in a world where others are constantly sizing up someone's outward projections to understand how to interact with them. From the inside, it can be confusing too. Most of us have mused aloud more than once, *I feel crazy,* in the midst of a massive transition where multiple feels come at us all at once.

It can be hard to make sense of at first, but with intention and awareness, you'll find understanding in your jumbled-together emotions coexisting as real. You don't have to choose one and reject another. Let what you feel come through. This is the messy truth of the in-between of grief. It's an *and* thing. All the feels come as they do, the joy and the pain, too. Once we create awareness around this truth, the felt permission follows and with it, the peace of allowing our experiences to unfold exactly as they are. No apology. No performance. No masks. No hiding or confusion. There is such relief in no longer needing to combat, outrun, and second-guess our every emotion. To learn to feel is the beginning of understanding what it is to heal.

WHAT YOU *CAN* DO

It's important to acknowledge before we go further that healing is not an all or nothing game. It is not an immediate and forever fix. Healing is not something that can be forced, charted, or achieved. There may be perspectives, choices and practices that you don't feel ready for. You may not be ready for them today or in ten months or ever. As we step through the chapters in this book, I'll be offering you more and more ways of looking at your grief experience and asking you to try on new ways of seeing, choosing, and living. What is asked of you in grief can feel like too much and as a result, you might feel yourself recoiling or rejecting it all. From here forward, let's simply look at the things you *can* do. Table the things that feel too big, too much, or too soon for another time. It can all feel overwhelming and that overwhelm can create anxiety. Anxiety is not the way to healing.

You may also wake up one day and realize that a certain practice suddenly feels intriguing. You may become inexplicably curious or drawn to something you never considered previously. That is your readiness coming through. That is the voice of knowing from deep inside whispering *Yes, maybe this, maybe now*. As you cultivate the practice of noticing what you notice, pay particular attention to your curiosity.

Curiosity tells us we're ready to come closer to an idea we don't know much about. Curiosity tells you it's safe to proceed, ask questions, gather data and maybe even try something new. This leads you to the pieces of the path to healing that you *can* do. Focus on those. In following your curiosity, you allow your experience to soften and become fluid. Curiosity allows you to let go of the outcome and find your way through the confusion of the in-between. In noticing what you notice, you allow your experience to simply unfold. This is the journey through grief.

HOW SOON IS TOO SOON?

My client Sandra came to me in a state of anxiety, tension and paralysis in the in-between. She felt like everything she chose was wrong. She told me she just *knew* everyone was watching and judging her every move. She was particularly wrapped up in the pain of what to do about his clothes still hanging in the closet. She was worried she'd be judged for clearing them out too soon and lamented over and over that she just knew *they* would all have something to say about it. I asked her if anyone had actually told her it was inappropriate and too soon after his death to put his clothes away. She paused and considered deeply for a moment before responding: *No.*

Then I asked her consider if it felt like the right time *for her* to take his clothes out of the closet. She smiled and I could hear her thoughts whirring before she answered. *It is! I know it is! I'm so tired of waking up every morning and seeing them still hanging there. My brain sees his clothes in there like they always were and it feels like I'm in my old life for half a second. Then I blink and have to remember he's dead again. It's going to be hard to touch it all, but I'm so ready to do something. I don't want to see them hanging there anymore. Somehow, it feels like I'm supposed to want to keep them there but I honestly don't. It hurts too much to look at them every day.*

Our conversation helped her see that only she could know what was right for her and on what timeline. Not only did she lovingly remove his clothes from her closet as a result of her new awareness and knowing, she took the next step too. Touching each belonging of his in her room, she intentionally chose what to keep for herself and donated the rest, offering some of his special things to those who appreciated them. She wakes up every morning in peace, free from the daily assault of pain and the fear of judgment too.

This is the core of moving through the in-between of grief. It takes intention and the willingness to notice what you notice. It takes courage to claim what you notice. Get curious enough about what you notice to understand what you need. Make an empowered choice that is right for you on the right timeline. Take action, not when it feels easy but when it feels right for you. This is where you begin. This is what you *can* do. This is moving through the in-between of grief.

REFLECTION

To navigate the wild and confusing in-between of grief, you'll find yourself becoming intentional with your grief. You'll draw closer to yourself and what you're really feeling. You'll start focusing on what you *can* do. Instead of judging what you notice, you'll understand it's simply showing you how best to proceed on the journey through grief. Free write what feels most true for you right now as you complete the prompts below:

- *When I notice what I notice, I know I feel...*
- *When I notice what I notice, I know I need...*
- *When I notice what I notice, I feel a connection to him in...*

- *When I notice what I notice, I still doubt myself when…*
- *When I notice what I noticed, I know I want to ask for…*

Chapter Four

Accessing Healing

I n this space of unraveling identities of wife, widow, and You, grief opens a direct access portal taking you straight to your core. Your truth becomes raw and more accessible here with no room for keeping up appearances and no energy for wearing masks. It's inside this raw space of grief that you learn to touch your pain to understand where healing must begin.

So often, the pain we access goes far beyond the excruciating ache of the husband we've buried; a lifetime of wounds collected awaiting healing. This next piece of the journey requires vulnerability and a willingness to dive layers and layers down into the real stuff of you. Nothing's hidden. It's no small task to look wholly into the hollows of unexplored soul space. The stillness and support of the chrysalis is necessary especially now as you examine deep wounds you thought were buried and long forgotten. The whole of you comes under the lens of examination; your wants, needs, and heartaches too. It is not a place to land, but a process to undergo.

UNDERSTANDING YOUR PAIN

Nigerian poet Ijeoma Umebinyuo says, "You must let the pain visit. You must allow it to teach you. You must not allow it to overstay." This takes great intention and careful awareness. You cannot skip past the deep ache to vitality. Nor can you force it away to begin with. You can only tend to it until it moves through, careful attention being paid to each wound as you rediscover them.

Inside this passage into vulnerability, you notice your fear of things like being *too much to love,* or *too emotional to be trusted.* You notice your belief that *you're just not good with money* or *you're too needy to ever do it alone.* The sharp words and unspoken reactions of those you loved cut deep enough once upon a time to rewrite your personal truth as one full of these limiting beliefs. These thoughts often come from an old page in your story yet they're influencing your journey through grief. They're shaping what you believe is true about your life as a widow. Whether you're aware of it or not, this old pain continues to inform your current reality, limiting the healing potential in your grief.

When we reencounter one of these old source stories—the ones these wounds and beliefs came from, we can be triggered.

It's no surprise there is resistance when this happens. Our survival center is activated once more, telling us to run. Now that you understand how to notice what you notice from the stable ground of the chrysalis, it's safer to look deep into the aches life has etched into your soul. When you're triggered and your pain is deepened, this is the moment when the vulnerability portal is most accessible to dive within. Only here do we have full access to tend to the wounds long awaiting healing. Until attention is paid, the ache will resurface over and over, demanding more attention each time like a festering infection that never heals.

NOTHING WORTH DOING IS EASY

The journey you're in the midst of is neither fast nor easy. What it will be is profound. What it will be is transformational. What it will be is uncomfortably vulnerable. What it will be is life changing. I'm inviting you to let go of your need for it to be easy. When you do, you will find more ease in the journey. There will be release as you discover what's there under the widow identity and the pain of grief. Layer by layer we shine the light of healing and release. The beautiful thing is you get to claim and hold onto the beautiful things you find down there too.

DEEPER THAN DEATH

Janessa felt like she was doing everything she was supposed to do in the name of healing. *I just feel hollow, no matter what I do,* she told me during one of our early calls together. We spent some time talking and on a hunch, I asked her *What are you most sad about?* Almost annoyed, she responded sharply about the obvious nature of her sadness. *My husband is dead. Sadness is all there is now. I miss him so of course I'm sad,* she almost snarled.

Knowing she had come far enough to access the portal of vulnerability, I inquired about another layer down. *What's below feeling sad about your husband's death?* I asked her. She got quiet for a long period of time before responding through gentle tears. *Fear. I'm afraid. I'm afraid of being a widow. I'm afraid of becoming the crazy person no one can stand to be around and eventually no one remembers. I'm afraid of becoming someone no one likes. I'm afraid of being lost in this grief. I'm afraid of being poor. I'm afraid of being someone no one ever loves again.*

There was relief in her voice as she said it aloud, acknowledging these deeper fears in herself for the first time. The vulnerability portal was wide open and she could finally see what was there. Of course, she was sad her husband was dead. The deep pain she was feeling was sourced by this undercurrent of limiting beliefs and fears she had accumulated about herself and what it meant to be a widow.

Janessa later shared about the experience of release she felt in naming these deeper sources of pain. *I can't explain it,* she told me. *I had no idea I was thinking about any of that. All the pain I was feeling was just directed toward missing him, I thought it was all about him. It feels weird to have misunderstood so much of my pain until now. But hearing myself say those words out loud made something click in me that I hadn't understood before. My pain is actually because of this other stuff. I still miss him, but the hurt is coming from even deeper than his death. Missing him feels different now that I know this.*

Janessa used the raw access to her own vulnerability to tap into a lifetime of inherited beliefs and wounds she didn't know were there. In our work together, we began examining the newfound understanding of her pain to understand how she could mentally shift some of her fears toward empowerment and peace where there was anxiety and pain. As a result, she began making choices that shifted her life in the same direction as her new beliefs. It was here that her lived suffering was alleviated. Her healing had begun.

FINDING YOUR WAY IN

We humans are not naturals at navigating and owning the depth of our emotions up and down the spectrum. We're particularly clumsy and resistant to moving toward the intensity and shadow of grief. So many times we have masked or stuffed our true experiences so people will continue to invite us into their world. We've lost so much already; the idea of losing friends and family because we're too far unraveled for them to stomach is more than we can bear.

I DON'T WANT TO BE THAT WIDOW

A client once lamented to me: *I don't want to be the widow who is always crying and always needy. Sometimes I just want to be the girl who is fun to be around. So, for a few hours, I put on a happy face and do my very best to be someone they want to be around. I can cry alone at home later. I'm afraid people will stop calling me. I don't want to be THAT widow.*

It won't be forever, but for now let yourself BE. Until you stop forcing your felt reality away, you cannot begin the journey into yourself. Allowing the scope of your experience to be fully felt by you and seen by those around you is the next task of healing. This is the way into the portal of vulnerability where true healing begins.

THE CURATOR

Julie's lifetime of shape-shifting to avoid judgment came to an all-time high in her life after loss. Using her go-to self-preservation mechanism, she became hyper-vigilant about projecting grace and honor in widowhood. Yes, she was hell-bent on getting her grief right, even with her therapist. Julie was feeling debilitating pain, yet she managed to exude strength due to a deeply engrained, powerful piece of her survival center: meet *the Curator*. We all have one, some calling upon her more than others in life. She seems to come to the forefront of our psyche when widowhood strikes, managing every decision for us with determination to protect us from further hurt inside our pain.

For as long as I can remember, Julie told me, *this Curator has been my go-to rep when I feel unsure about how to navigate painful parts of my life.* She explained the exact feeling she'd get in her body when the voice of the curator was overriding her reality to keep her safe. *It's almost like I am outside my body watching myself go through the motions,* she said. Julie said she would watch herself smiling, nodding, and saying the right words in conversations she was feeling pain from. *I would be thanking this person for the unhelpful things they were saying, and I'm dying on the inside, mostly waiting for it to be over,* Julie told me.

THE UNWRITTEN RULES EVERYONE KNOWS

Whether anyone wants to acknowledge it, we're here to say it out loud: there are rules we each have internalized about how to live in life after loss and how to grieve with honor and dignity. We all grow up absorbing what's acceptable and allowable in our unique social contexts when it comes to grief and expressing emotions. The *Curator* is like a tether, reminding us what a "good" widow does even when she's exhausted and aching on the inside.

Becoming aware of your *Curator* is a fascinating experience because it helps you see just how often you give up control and allow her to smooth over your seemingly out of control existence. It helps you project poise, confidence, and graciously receive all the gestures and comments others offer that aren't always helpful.

When I noticed my own personal curator it made me curious about who was stepping aside to make space for her to take center stage. *Who was I really? What was I really feeling? What did I really want to say and why wasn't I saying it? What did I really need? How many times had I abandoned my truth in the name of trying to be ok, or strong, or graceful?* What *Madame Curator* was doing was stripping my vulnerability and painting over it with an impenetrable triple sealed coating of high gloss self-preservation.

Unfortunately, when the *Curator* keeps our vulnerability and truth at bay in the name of *protecting us*, she's limiting our healing potential, too. Behind her work, there's a lingering knowing that something powerful is missing from our lives. It often shows up as a hollow feeling inside and can be accompanied by a lethargy of sorts, among other manifestations. It takes time and intentional practice to notice the *Curator* when she shows up and a whole load of courage to ask her to step aside to allow your authentic experiences to unfold without filter, performance, or masquerade.

NO MORE MAKING NICE WITH EXPECTATION

Something powerful shifts at this point in the journey through grief. Once consumed by playing your *role* as widow, you now come to understand that it's your lived experience that matters and those who love you will support your journey, come what may. With the newfound awareness that the *Curator* exists in each of us, we become more aware of our ability to identify and communicate the truth of our experience rather than playing along to get it right. Once you tap into your truth, perspective shows you how much more discomfort there is in going unseen in the name of playing it safe. There is liberation in letting go of the need to conform to the way you think you *should* be, and exist as you *are*.

SHE'S JUST GRIEVING

Your old tribe is quite often baffled by who you're becoming without the direction of the *Curator*. However full of love and well-intentioned this old tribe may be, they do not know the new you who's taking form within the chrysalis. Let's be honest, you barely do! They're waiting for the old you to come back from *grief-land* one day when you find closure. *I'm glad you're getting better*, they say, as though you're recovering from the measles. *I'm glad you're moving on*, as though all you have to do is simply forget the pain. They write off any unusual new ways of being, living, and feeling as you "just grieving," a temporary and particular type of insanity similar to a mid-life crisis. I experienced this "pat on the head" response over and over. At first, it stung and made me feel small. Once I realized how little it mattered, it felt like breaking free. I was finding my way home to *me*.

With much practice and awareness, you'll gradually be more at ease expressing your vulnerable truths than the sanitized platitudes of the party line to protect yourself from judgment. There will be times when you'll feel safer keeping it to yourself, but no longer will you tolerate what agonizes you on the inside. You'll become skilled at discerning who your safe people are. You'll become better at choosing who you do (and more importantly do NOT) spend your time and energy with.

Your safe inner circle becomes your closest and likely much smaller tribe. These are your go-to humans who know how to stand beside you in your storm and on sunny days too. Do you know what happens when your *Curator* hops in the backseat and lets you drive? Your safe people (and even some unexpected ones on the fringe of your inner circle) show up with you differently! In sharing your true experience and getting vulnerable and real, you offer permission for others to do the same. It makes them feel safe to come closer to you and stand inside the storm beside you.

CLAIMING YOUR HUMANNESS

Navigating this piece of the journey is about looking ahead while honoring where you have been and what's happening in the present too. This is a call to tenderly excavate your personal belief system and lifetime of wounds in an intentional way that brings clarity, peace of mind, and release of thought patterns that create suffering. You didn't bring about the tragedy that has brought you to the depths on your knees, but you have so much more choice and healing potential in the way ahead than you've been allowed to believe. Finding your way through the pain requires you to first walk through the fire toward the place where you touch the wound. Perhaps the most crucial element of the journey through grief is allowing our raw, unfiltered humanness to come through.

REFLECTION

To truly step into being powerfully vulnerable, I want you to think about the times you've hidden or chosen to override your real emotions or thoughts in the name of projecting an image of being OK. I'm talking about all the times you've continued to show up in the world other than as you really are. Can you envision what life would feel like without the need to perform? No pretense. No projection. No performance. Bringing yourself powerfully whole and unfiltered to your experience, without the direction of the *Curator* protecting you, is what truly allows you to begin moving toward the direction of forward. Think of some times your inner world and outer world have not been in alignment. Free write what feels most true for you right now as you complete the prompts below:

- *I often hide my pain by…*
- *I often protect myself from vulnerability because…*
- *I often feel I have to be strong when…*
- *I feel ready to admit that…*

Chapter Five

Moving Forward Isn't Letting Go

You don't mean to, but you notice the timeline of your every story is measured from the date of his death. Your entire life is suddenly laid out as what happened before he died and the pain that came after. Some days, you secretly hope your broken heart will never heal because you're afraid you'll have to forget in order to truly live again. You're terrified that moving forward is the same as leaving him behind and you'll never be *over* loving him. You would rather feel the pain of grief than ever give up the claim to continue loving him. You accept this either/or scenario of grieving or living and choose his memory over the second-best kind of life without him you're capable of imagining.

KEEP YOUR LOVE STORY

The truth is you never have to abandon your love story in the name of healing. Everything about who he was is yours to love forever. The story you co-created with the man you buried belongs to you always. Both the pages of the life you shared and the experience of his death are woven deeply into the fabric of your story now. Just as your childhood memories and teenage misadventures are an integral part of who you've become, so too is the piece of your story that happened with him. It's yours. He's yours. Always and forever, this dance you shared is yours to remember, love, cherish and honor. What comes next is too. You never have to give up the part of your story that came before he died to open to what comes next.

HE WAS MY EVERYTHING

Patrice had dedicated her six years of widowhood to honoring her late husband's life every way she could find. She spent most of our first call telling me of her deep devotion to the love story she had shared with him, outlining the extensive list of memorials she had coordinated or participated in and the grief support groups she attended simply to have a place to talk about him. She did share that she didn't particularly enjoy the groups, but said *it was the right thing to do.* In the very next moment, she shared how exhausted she was. She felt like she had nothing to live for. She was so tired and so lonely. She had so many things she wanted to do but just couldn't bring herself to begin. *After this much time, it's like everyone else has moved on with their lives. He was my everything. I can't do that to him too,* she told me.

During that same conversation, I gently shared with Patrice the flipside to her limiting belief; that living a life of joy after loss didn't have to mean forgetting him. Her tears began to fall almost immediately and it was a few minutes before she was able to explain. *After all these years,* she said, *it is such a relief to hear you say that. I can't believe it's that simple but it finally clicked. I've been terrified of abandoning him. My life has felt so small since he died, but I couldn't bring myself to choose happiness again if it meant leaving him behind.*

Becoming aware of her fear of having to forget him to heal was all she needed to move into a more intentional grief, and intentional living for that matter, too. Patrice was eyes-wide-open for the first time since her late husband's death and she was actually feeling excitement, something she told me she had long since given up on ever feeling again. She was suddenly inspired and feeling more full of peace than ever too. She didn't have to take down the pictures of him in her home or take off her wedding ring to begin. She started by planning a summer of travel to several places she'd always dreamed of visiting; a trip she hadn't considered honorable to do without him previously. She got to keep her love story and begin learning to love her life after loss, too. Through her ability to notice what she was afraid of, she was able to release her fear and move forward in her journey through grief.

UNFINISHED BUSINESS

There's a less romantic piece of honoring your love story that's important to acknowledge. In the in-between of grief, you may find your story being painted rose colored by the people around you. A very human part of honoring our dead is remembering them larger than life. More often than not, death makes them heroes and we tell only the glory stories. We keep the less pretty, less perfect, more painful pieces of their humanness tucked away. We protect their honor and sometimes in doing so, we're protecting ours, too. So often in the performance of the funeral, a picture of our person gets painted that doesn't always match the full scale of your shared truth. Right or wrong, our culture chooses to memorialize their perfection and slide under the rug their very real human vulnerabilities that affected the dance you shared, sometimes in deeply painful ways.

You may have the most gorgeous love story full of romance and tenderness with pockets full of picturesque images telling your tale. You may have the most painful, complicated love story, full of unfinished conversations and pieces of resentment or worse in your grief. If you're deeply honest, your story was likely a mix of the two because even a great love story is messy and full of peaks, valleys and plateaus. You're allowed to honor the reality of your story and often that brings with it layers upon layers of stories to celebrate and grieve all the more deeply. You remember the fight you had just days before he died. You wish you had loved him harder and told him so more. You lament not taking the trip and making a big deal out of the vacuuming that never got done. You long for another chance to forgive and mean it.

None of this makes your grief any less yours to feel. None of this makes your love any less true. Remember it all as it actually was, not as you've been asked to paint it for the consumption of others as you grieve. There is nothing uncomplicated about grief, so grieve the real-for-you story that died with him. Not everyone will know that version of the story, but it gets to be true for you. This takes us back to acknowledging the reality of where you are; the intentional grief that helps you move beyond the in-between. Until you claim and address the whole truth of the story you're grieving, that hurt will remain. You get to decide who you do or don't share it with, but the regrets and still open wounds of the real stories are begging to be acknowledged in the in-between spaces of your pain.

CULTIVATING ACCESS

A foundational piece of intentional grief that brings so much peace to this in-between stage is the way we acknowledge signs and connections with spirit. Noticing what you notice once again comes into play here. Your beliefs about what happens to someone when the physical body dies inform your grief deeply. So often, we in Western culture see the finality of life in terms of physical form: you're either here on earth or you're gone, an accepted separation between the realms of life on earth and the great beyond. So many of us deep in grief grapple with profound encounters with spirit, something we've assigned so much meaning to and often refused to see.

On the one hand, these experiences are deeply comforting as we feel viscerally a presence, connection or communion with the person we are mourning. On the other hand, our lifetime of cultural learning has told us that we're either crazy or simply imagining what cannot be. It's so easy to dismiss these sacred encounters as seeing what we want to see. I want to challenge you to notice what you notice about the thin veil that connects us to them beyond death. It's not important where you think they go after death, it's important what you notice. In noticing what you notice, you'll learn to cultivate access to him in ways you might not have previously believed and as a result, might not have been able to receive. This doesn't make you psychic, telepathic, or clairvoyant necessarily (unless you want it to), it simply makes you a human with the awareness to notice what you notice and not make it wrong.

We struggle so much to explain the synchronistic events we witness throughout our lives. What if we simply noticed that some particularly vibrant sunsets make us feel closer to our dead husband than we can explain? In the first months after his death, it seemed each sunset was a nod and a smile from my late husband telling me to carry on; that he was going to make sure everything turned out OK. I felt it so deeply in my body, as though he was holding me in an embrace. I decided to simply embrace it. Instead of making myself crazy for experiencing it that way or pathetic, even, for needing it, I simply allowed myself to feel that squeeze of my hand from him in the form of a sunset. I went so far as to tell my kids about those particular sunsets as gifts from him. *Your daddy painted this one for you,* I'd say. Because I gave them permission to experience the sunset that way too, they simply smile and say, *Thanks daddy!* The connection is cultivated. What a gift to continue experiencing his support and acts of love that way. It doesn't make me needy. It doesn't make me new age. Regardless of where I believe "he" is right now beyond the grave, I know I experience him often in the form of a sunset.

USE THE ANIMALS

One of my clients told me the most beautiful story that gave me goose bumps as she described it. She said: *As my grandfather was saying his goodbyes from his hospice bed, I asked him to use animals to communicate with us. He paused for a moment and then nodded and replied, "Alright." Just a few days after he died, my grandma was looking out the sliding doors like she had done so many times before, usually watching birds and squirrels. A deer walked across her yard and stood quietly at the sliding doors, looking into the living room. The deer was so purposeful and calm. My uncle was there and walked up to the sliding door and even opened it. The deer didn't budge. When my uncle stepped out of the house, the deer sauntered off slowly. Once he went back inside, the dear once again approached the sliding doors. It was as though he was looking inside.*

I feel crazy, she said, *but what are the odds of that happening soon after our conversation about using animals to interact with us after he died? It made me feel so happy and so connected to him, even in the possibility. It made me uncomfortable and it made me feel a little crazy too. Am I just seeing what I want to see? I'm a Christian; it feels wrong somehow to believe something more about what sounds like a wild coincidence to everyone else.*

SYNCHRONICITY AND WHAT IS REAL?

The final piece to cultivating access in encounters with spirit is making it tangible in written form, if only for yourself. When you experience a moment of synchronicity or a message from spirit, no matter how brief, consider writing it down. It's easy to stand in awe for a moment with a felt connection and the next moment brush it off as ridiculous. However, when you sit with a notebook full of experiences and messages and synchronicities you've recorded, it makes seeing the access you've experienced with him even beyond the grave very real. You simply notice what you notice and write it down when you do. This list becomes a reminder of the ongoing connection with him that is always yours so long as you remain open to receiving it.

The only thing that stands between profound experiences with spirit is simply our willingness to receive. You're not believing *in* anything, you're simply allowing yourself to notice what you notice and feel what you feel. All it takes is a commitment to noticing without judgment. There's no magical, deep spiritual practice on this one. You simply notice how the song you hear everywhere you go feels like him saying hello. And so it is. You simply notice that when you find a special-to-him item seemingly out of place itfeels like an *I love you* message at a moment when you needed it most. And so it is. In cultivating this access from the in-between of grief, you find you're more ready to begin taking those small steps on the journey through grief. With the connection to your someone strong beyond the grave, you find yourself empowered to move forward in the knowing the connection will always be there between you.

DREAMS AS MEDICINE

A similar lens can be applied to what we experience in dreams. Endless clients suffering in the confusing in-between of grief have shared stories of vivid dreams. These powerfully real remembered dreams about people we love deeply who are no longer living are often accompanied by fear because they violate so much of the certainty about what is real as we've been taught to understand it. *It was just a dream.* Much like everyday miracles, we dismiss our potent dreams as benign. *Just dreams.* We treat our dreams as meaningless background noise, like the reality TV show playing behind our closed eyes as we sleep. We have enough science now to study and measure how there is so much more psychic work being done in the deep sleep of dreaming than we've given credit to. We can measure brain waves and physiology and the healing of traumas being facilitated as we sleep.

To those dreaming the lucid dreams with their deceased beloved person, I say: notice what you notice and take from it what you need. *They feel so real,* they tell me. *It's literally as though I'm right there with him in physical form. He smells exactly right. He's wearing the clothes that are still hanging in the closet. I'm able to touch him and he feels just like he did.* Often they tell me they couldn't speak. Many say they just looked at their beloved in dreaming and cried.

Even in dreaming, you notice what you notice. You cultivate access further by keeping a journal by your bedside to record the details of the dream as you're able to recall them before you fully wake. If you have ceased dreaming, be kind to yourself and go gently and invite the dreams to come when the time is right. From the in-between of grief, dreams can act as medicine. By bringing intention to our awareness around our dreams, we can experience both another thread of connection to them beyond this physical plane and play out some deep processing of grief's pain too. Dreams offer us insight, information, connection, and a safe space for healing in the in-between of grief.

CLAIMING YOUR TRUTH

So much of our suffering comes from the need to dismiss the very real experience of our grief, not just the tough to talk about emotions, but the moments of synchronicity and connection to spirit too. It's common for others to have a hard time understanding the value you place on these experiences, should you choose to share them. When we claim and cultivate the connection to spirit and dreaming in life after loss, we move beyond the in-between of grief where confusion and disconnect reign into a place of knowing, powerful vulnerability, and peace.

REFLECTION

When you consider your journey through grief, what role has fear of forgetting him played in that experience? So often, we grasp tightly to them in memories and physical objects, as though trying desperately to keep the truth of him from slipping through our fingers entirely like grains of sand that cannot be contained. So often in death, we fear our connection to them is lost altogether. Consider your journey and take a moment to remember some moments of fear and also some of synchronicity. Free write what feels most true for you right now as you complete the prompts below:

- *The most important things to remember about him are...*
- *I'm afraid of forgetting him because...*
- *I'm afraid if I one day find myself no longer painfully grieving, it means...*

- *What makes me feel most connected to him after his death is…*
- *A time when I experienced synchronistic events that felt like a connection to him was…*
- *A meaningful dream involving him that I can remember felt…*

Chapter Six

Permission To Live

G rief support is so often about creating a community where those deep in grief gather to commiserate and survive. It's a brilliant idea to bring together people who can truly understand and empathize with one another in a way those who haven't experienced grief seem unable to. The problem is, within these support circles where the common thread is grief, suffering is generally accepted as a terminal diagnosis for the bereaved, a place to stay.

So often, we're not ready to hold another's pain for them or with them as we're wading through our own. It becomes overwhelming and so often it can easily become a place of commiseration. An unintended consequence of these support spaces for grieving hearts is that they can solidify our expectations and fears of what it means to be a widow. Gathered together, I found people who were years and years into their journey with grief, and appeared to be just as devastated as I felt in those initial months. I didn't judge their process, but I hoped in my soul that my life didn't still feel enveloped by pain after a decade of time gone by. Something deep inside me told me it didn't have to be.

LET'S TALK ABOUT LIVING

There were workshops on stress management. There were meetings about survival skills and coping strategies. There were ample opportunities to honor my dead husband. Literally no one was talking about healing or living. There were no inspirational speakers. The message was continually about a place to connect with people who understood our suffering, a place where we could safely remember the dead and acknowledge grief's everlasting pain together. Everything was about honoring and remembering *them*. I was comforted by the solidarity I found in the knowing I wasn't the only one living in deep grief and hearing the heart wrenching stories of others certainly allowed me the perspective to cultivate gratitude for the support I had at the ready. Yet, every resource seemed to coax me closer to the stereotype of merely surviving life I hoped I didn't have to become.

RECLAIM YOUR IDENTITY

It's fascinating the way we identify with our limitations in modern culture. Instead of saying we are struggling with our weight, we claim it: *I am obese.* Instead of making diabetes a medical diagnosis, we claim it: *I am a diabetic.* Even in mourning, the bereaved take it on: *I am a widow. I am a surviving spouse.* They even give us a whole separate box to check on intake forms. Words can erase us from existence and assign us a whole new identity, simple identifying words literally locking us away inside them. We're slowly becoming more conscious about this in terms of gender and race but we're missing the mark entirely when it comes to relationship status, medical status, educational status and more. These words carry rules about what is allowed for the person they describe. These words are limiting and create separation instead of connection.

When you *identify* as someone else's widow, the word literally puts their life's value before yours. When you *identify* as someone's survivor, your worth in the world is validated by the fact that they existed and you are now left behind. It inherently strips *you* of your worth to exist independent of him and the cultural norms that are permanently attached to those words. Language choice allows the neuropathways of your personal belief systems to adapt to a different set of truths when practiced with intention. Your words can solidify your expectation of and dedication to a lifetime of suffering. Your words can equally solidify empowerment and hope in the story of your life still being written.

You are you. You've been a lot of things to a lot of people, among them is a wife to your late husband. None of these old roles are washed away by the word widow, but neither is all that you will become. There is so much life yet for you to live and the only limitations to the story of what comes next will be put there by you.

The ultimate act of vulnerability is stripping yourself of attachments to identities, learning to exist and be valued *just* as yourself. We're going head to head with the system here and I'll be the first to acknowledge it. I'm offering you permission you don't actually need to take a step toward reclamation of something you haven't realized you'd been asked to give up. When you choose to hang up your identity as widow right beside your identity as wife, you keep those pieces of your story and honor the fact that no choice you make in the present could diminish the beautiful chapters behind you. Yet, you begin to create space for your Self and who she's becoming at this point in the journey through grief too.

FIND YOUR TRIBE

Finding a powerful group of humans who are willing to walk beside you inside this vulnerable journey through grief empowers you to live and express the truths you're collecting there. There may be family members and people from your life before he died who choose to stay by your side that will become elemental to your healing journey. There will likely be new friends you find in life after loss, too.

They'll be the ones you feel safe to be truly seen by. They'll be the ones who try to understand. They'll show up again and again. They'll hold sacred what you notice and need. They'll know you don't need to be fixed or saved. They'll know when it's time to dance beside you and cry with you when it's time for that too. They'll understand grief is an *and* thing and they'll be up for the vulnerability it takes to stay by your side. These people will empower you again and again to carry on the journey of unraveling to become who you will in your life after loss.

BOUNDARIES

There will likely be times when thoughtless comments and unwelcome counsel leaves you feeling irresponsible, incapable, and irrational in your journey through grief. There may even be moments when others demonstrate somewhat aggressively the urgency they feel to save you from yourself. There will be some expecting you to sooner or later *get over it* so you can go back to being the *normal* you they remember you being. There will be some well-intentioned people whose interpretation of your relationship becomes vastly more emotionally intimate than it ever was prior to your grief. Your desire to maintain boundaries that feel safe and true to you is always yours to choose, regardless of how others interpret their realities.

Most of these people will believe they know what's best for you, even more than you do and they'll be bound and determined to either fix you or help you save yourself from your grief. These people will come in all forms: family, friends, medical professionals, clergy. Even strangers will want to weigh in on what's right for you, often explaining their sister's brother's veterinarian's loss and somehow relating it to yours, if only to offer solidarity in that *they* know how you feel. It is deeply important to remember that of these people, not one of them has ever been you. They have never lived, let alone grieved deeply, inside the unique circumstances that make up the reality of life as you know it.

Remember that in every case, you get to choose whose advice and insights you listen to. You get to choose whose energies and beliefs you receive and retain. You get to choose who you say yes to. You always get to decline a gesture offered in support that lands with unintended pain. You are allowed to practice saying *No, thank you,* guilt-free. You can ignore their stories and suggestions completely. You decide what you keep. You determine the boundaries and teach people how they're allowed to interact with you in a way that feels safe and is actually supportive and decline the rest.

HEAR WHAT THEY MEAN

You learn the power of choosing to hear them attempting to say "I love you and I care," when the actual words of those around you land a different way in grief. In doing so, you do not take on the pain they've unintentionally delivered. You're never required to receive their fumbled attempts at love when it comes out as painful projections or unsolicited advice. Instead, you set aside energetically whatever they've offered you that doesn't land with comfort, connection, or ease. You can simply say to yourself, *I know they're coming with the kindest of loving intentions. I choose to hear them saying "I love you," instead of what actually came out of their mouth.*

It's incredible how this has allowed me the presence to more carefully communicate what my boundary is in that moment and help them see the type of support that would (if any) feel better than what they provided. Sometimes, a simple *thank you for thinking of me* is enough to gracefully complete the exchange if that feels safer than a lesson on empathy, or vulnerability.

You always retain permission to set and maintain the energetic, verbal, and physical boundaries that feel safe to interact with others from within.

LIVING FROM YOUR SHOULDS

When it comes to reclaiming identity and upholding boundaries at this juncture in the journey through grief, it can feel unsettling to find yourself so wholly situated within the truth of you with no other filter or imagined rulebook as guide. It takes great intention to pay attention to your truths, wants, and needs above the perceived expectations you've been living from. I can hear you wondering: *So, where do I begin living? How will I know what's real and what's just me protecting myself? Nothing feels true anymore. I don't even know what I need.*

When you really notice what you notice about how you're spending your life and with whom, you will see the enormous multi-layered filter of *should* you've been running most of it through. We do this in womanhood. We do this in motherhood. We do this in widowhood. We create a set of rules and limitations that are simply stories we tell ourselves about what's allowable and safe in our life after loss.

Permission granted to rewrite the script. Come back to noticing what you notice, but this time pay attention to where you are living from your *shoulds*, the source of so much suffering. Notice what you choose, and more importantly, notice if you're choosing it because you *think* you *should*. Eliminate anything that starts with the phrase *I think I should* and replace it with *I choose to*. Notice what you notice about what you choose and when you get body-slammed by a *should*.

You've always got permission to choose. You've always got permission to change your mind. This is where your life after loss becomes yours to live.

DO NOT BE AFRAID

From where you sit inside your grief, I acknowledge it likely feels like this can't possibly be true for you. *My pain is too deep and you couldn't understand,* I hear you saying. I know that's where your thoughts are because they were once mine too. I once thought all the *it will be different someday* chatter was all fairy tales and platitudes, too. Author Elizabeth Gilbert spun me back to a place of knowing when I heard her say, "When you reach the end of yourself, you can either die into despair or surrender into divinity. When you ask the question *who am I?* or *who is God?* you will end up at the same place. At the bottom of every mystical journey, you find a small voice that says: *Do not be afraid.*" Die into despair or surrender into divinity. Permission granted: you choose.

OPEN TO POSSIBILITY

It's true, grief will have its own story and unique timing for each one of us touched to the core by the death of someone we love. I beg you to honor your journey and know there's more to the experience of grief than pain and suffering. Your authentic experience won't look exactly like the movies or behave like you think it should if you can find your way beyond expectation, judgment, and fear. The depth and duration of your pain is not what honors the man whose death you grieve, your life does. I'm not asking you to bypass your pain, as if you could.

I'm asking you to give up the rules you've created about what life after loss is supposed to look like. I'm asking you to open to possibility.

A SWEETNESS YOU CAN'T IMAGINE

The man you love is no longer living, but *your story* is still being written, every day another page. Right now, it might feel like it's being written around you, maybe even over you. It feels like you're waist-deep in quicksand, clawing and scratching your way through with nothing solid to cling to. Life without him beside you right now feels empty, surreal, and suffocating but something more does come next. Beyond the journey through grief is the rest of your life and it's sweeter than anything you could imagine until you one day find yourself there and take in the life of your new dreams. I want you to know there is something more to choose if you have the courage to claim it. The only way you'll know you're ready is to begin. Remember, you're not doing this alone. Read on, sister.

REFLECTION

On this journey through grief, we access healing when we give ourselves permission to do so. We do this by releasing limiting beliefs and identities that have left us feeling trapped inside a life of *shoulds*. We do this by drawing strength from the tribe who walks beside us and by holding boundaries to help the rest understand how best they can show up with us. Take a few moments to think about where you've been wishing for permission to move forward in your life after loss. Are you ready to give yourself that permission? Free write what feels most true for you right now as you complete the prompts below:

- *The grief resources that feel empowering and helpful are...*
- *I feel most safe and seen when someone...*
- *A boundary that is important to me in grief is...*

Chapter Seven

Mastering Your Reality

Here is where we truly depart from the grief story we've been told in every Hollywood fable and cautionary tale about what happens to widows when their husbands die. This is where we leave behind the belief system we grew up with that the suffering of grief lasts a lifetime. This is where we move deep into the vulnerability we've worked so hard to access. This is where we uncover what's there and slowly move beyond the devastation that your husband's death brought toward all that's yet to come. This is where we conduct an inquiry around what's actually true and possible in life after loss and reject the limiting beliefs creating so much pain.

THE HUNT FOR CLARITY

It's time to explore and better understand the often-misrepresented journey through grief. What does it even *mean* to grieve actively and intentionally? When does grief become a verb instead of a thing you're overcome by? You've come here looking for clarity and maybe even hope as you find your way along the path. To find what you seek, we'll practice identifying the limiting beliefs that are sources of pain, suffering, and often immobilizing in the way ahead. It's very likely you don't even know they are there. We often accept them as *truths* dressed as emotions and feelings and sometimes realistic fears. Believe me, those limiting beliefs in each of us are many and they are vast. That they exist within you means nothing more than this: you are both fully human and alive. Without negating the ache of grief for him, there's so much in your head and heart that can be released to alleviate the additional suffering you're carrying and create space for peace, relief and even living.

THE WORK

One of the most profoundly revealing practices you can use for healing comes from a deep examination of your thoughts. Byron Katie is a luminary whose work revolves around the simple fact that our suffering comes from arguing with reality. Nowhere more than in grief do we argue, and even beg for what's real to be untrue. How many times have you pleaded to wake up from the nightmare and find that he wasn't really dead? Byron Katie's "The Work" leads you to see just how limiting the beliefs you are so deeply committed to actually are. Sometimes these beliefs have been made into a personal truth long ago in childhood and have informed your life for so long you don't even know it's happening. Being led through her process of inquiry that facilitates deep release and processing in a gentle and unforced way can change reality as you know it. As you identify a painful belief (that often *feels* very real), you walk through a process that helps you see it for what it is: a belief. Beliefs have no power; they come from thoughts with no roots in reality. You have the power to change your thoughts and beliefs and her process helps you see how the opposite of your painful belief could be just as true or truer. There's no forcing, there's simply a profound shift in perspective you can actually *feel* aligning in your body. There is peace where there was turmoil, a release of suffering every time!

LANGUAGE

On the topic of leaning into the acceptance of reality, we come back around full circle to language and understanding its power. In his TedxDirigo talk, Phuc Tran riffed on grammar and language as "your first and most powerful tool," and in my work I couldn't agree more. He specifically discusses the subjunctive and indicative and the pitfalls of each. The subjunctive, Tran says, "allows us to look into the past and imagine what could have (or should have) happened." He goes on to say that those whose language lacks the subjunctive possess a way of seeing that is "fundamental to resiliency without expending psychic energy on what could have been." It turns out, countries whose language lacks the subjunctive tense are exponentially happier than those with it. The reason for this is simple: without the subjunctive, the speaker is unable to "obsess over what could have been," as Tran put it. Thinking and communicating purely from the indicative, Phuc Tran closes with, "allows us to talk about ourselves and our experience in real terms, especially if we have the courage to embrace that reality." Goodness, oh so much of our grief exploration and healing process revolves around that very courageous act of embracing our new reality.

REJECTING VICTIM MENTALITY

Sometimes we make ourselves the victim. Sometimes others see us as such. There's no lack of pity projected onto us in widowhood, particularly in the early weeks when everyone's focus is on us. We take on their death as something that happened to us, something that *means* something about us, and something we must suffer. We become the victim of their death and we are given words that we take on as identity about what that victimhood means about who we will become and how we will live and feel about it all. Trauma resolution educator Rachel Maddox observes that from within victim mentality, "we don't have a connection to choice." It all just *is*. We, as widows, believe ourselves to be the victims of what happened and so we trudge on, adhering to the rules we've both created and accepted about the way things *are* and the way things must always be as a widow. Accepting your victim status in grief is like being bound and tethered to your pain. Your whole worldview revolves around how this shouldn't have happened to you. It's a horribly tragic thing to experience the death of someone you love, but the fact is: it *did* happen.

It happened inside your story. The one thing we can know for sure about life is that one day, we all will die. Making yourself a victim of life's one guaranteed truth ensures you'll remain married to pain.

ACCEPTANCE IS NOT THE SAME AS SETTLING

There's a fear that when you stop arguing with reality, it means you're accepting this second best life that feels so empty and all the pain that comes with it. A client said to me once: *It feels like accepting this means I'm settling. Shouldn't I be trying harder to get out of it? How can I ever be happy again if I accept this horrible ending to my love story? Doesn't it take effort and pushing through the pain of reality to heal? Accepting this feels worse than working hard to get away from it. Aren't I risking depression if I don't take my life into my own hands?*

My client and I worked together over the course of several weeks to see that accepting what is true alleviates the need to do anything other than experience it as it comes and choose how to respond to what is real and *only* to that. When we stop pushing it away and allow it to be, we are more able to notice what we're really afraid of and choose accordingly a more safe path. We're able to notice what we need to feel safe and nurtured inside our reality and create boundaries and opportunities to feel more of that. We notice what we can choose that feels empowering inside our reality. We notice that when we stop making our reality mean something about us, we are free. Slowly the pain relinquishes its iron grip and we move into living with more ease. There is freedom in accepting our reality. From this place, we can begin living with intention.

IS CLOSURE REAL?

Some believe closure means you've gotten answers to why it all had to happen the way it did. They believe when they know why, they'll be fine and they keep waiting. They keep begging to know: *Why him? Why then? Why us? Why not me?* I don't believe there is an answer to *why*. I think closure happens through accepting "what is". We arrive to a place where there is a profound internalization that he *is* dead, that his physical body no longer *is* him. No longer is there pleading for it not to be so (which I hope goes without saying doesn't mean we're happy it happened, we're just no longer grappling with the facts). Instead of being swallowed whole by the widow identity, we learn to reclaim our journey and experience life as it is without measuring against what we think it should be.

Closure comes when we give up arguing with reality and make peace with what has been. I think the ongoing suffering comes from our demanding an answer to "why" and waiting in earnest for it one day to come. We abandon a possibility of healing when we choose to believe we can never truly heal without knowing *why*. Letting go of needing to know why allows us to process more deeply what was true and move from there. It's not a thing you can force or want hard enough to happen. It's part of the process. It's part of the journey. It's part of the necessity of grief. Every bit of felt pain and processing is a piece of the path to closure.

There's a belief that we'll have made it through grief when we "get closure." When I asked my client Lynne about closure, she said: *No, I don't believe there will ever be closure but oddly enough I think I still went looking for it. In the beginning I felt like I had to do all these things perfectly and get them done to "finish". But I realized I was doing them because somewhere in my mind if I did them "right" he would still come back to me.*

Our culture as a whole seems to think closure is when grief is "finished," but of course it doesn't work that way. Ashley Davis Bush is a social worker who wrote, "transcending loss is the process of learning to live with love and loss side by side in a way that brings greater meaning and purpose into our lives." It's interesting to ask people what the word "closure" means to them, as there are a lot of views on the topic. In general, it all comes back to being OK. We seem to collectively believe closure means someone is "all better." With that belief comes an air of forgetting or "moving on," and an underlying abandonment of the entire thing. Somehow this is the model that we accept as true healing. I challenge this with the nuance of language and its power. To me, the concept of "closure" is fluid and generally has more to do with heart and soul than it does with choices you make in your life after loss. Getting remarried does not mean someone has closure. Just as, someone who lives in the same home she built with her late husband thirty years after his death might absolutely have closure. It's simply a truth. Someone with closure is no longer triggered to pain by the reality of death. It doesn't mean you've forgotten. You don't "get over it" or "move on," you *move forward*. You live life in the present, refusing to allow what you choose in the now to negate the beauty of what has been your past.

ALWAYS LONELY BUT NEVER ALONE

A dear client named Catie told me, "I'm always lonely and NEVER alone." This is something so many women I've supported, myself included, have said approximately one million times about life after loss. Many of these women are mothers and spend much of their time caring for little ones even while deeply in grief. Those without children have expressed envy for the way having children gives you an urgency to press on and heal. Those with children have expressed envy for having no children and therefore no one to care for but yourself while grieving. It is clear there is pain in both sides of the story.

As a mother of four children under 6 when my husband died, I can say that even when I was with grown-ups, so often I felt alone. Almost as a rule, whether friend or stranger, they couldn't really see me or understand my pain and I didn't feel safe to show them. One client shared this thought many seem to relate with: *I've actually had to push friends and family away just so I can be alone. I don't mind being alone, it allows me to feel my true feelings. When I am with people, I am numb. I know many friends and family are watching me, worried about me and for me, but I hate knowing I am being watched and pitied.*

Being alone doesn't hurt less in grief, but sometimes choosing it on occasion can feel more true than performing for people with whom you feel the need to filter out the truth of you. When choosing to be alone feels like too much, look to that inner circle to hold space for you. Not just anyone will do in loneliness. Allow yourself permission to be selective about who you call on for companionship in the most intense times of loneliness.

trying to make sense of their experience by observing ours, we find ourselves in a personal reality that feels unsafe. *I'm trying so hard to be OK*, I've been told over and over by clients desperate to escape the pain. This *trying* activates physiological responses inherent to our survival center. Our body and our thoughts literally respond to our lived and expressed grief as a threat to our personal safety and survival. One of the most profound and truly human experiences we will encounter has been made the villain. We cast off our grief in the name of saving ourselves, only to unknowingly reject the painful path so necessary for healing.

PAIN IN THE MEMORIES

Grief's lurking shadow is always there now it seems, plunging you into pain with every step. Tears linger at the surface. Every smell, song, space, and dream contains a memory of what is no longer yours to hold. The clothes in the closet, the boxes in the hall, even the mail reminds you of who's missing. Your broken heart is bombarded by remnants of a happy life everywhere you turn. Beautiful nostalgia has become the twisting knife in a painful wound you can barely withstand. And yet, you're terrified you might one day forget it all, too, and so you cling even more tightly to the memories despite the pain.

Some days you imagine running away from the wreckage and never looking back. Sometimes you dream of being rescued by another love story you don't actually believe in or want. You ache to honor him and do right by your love story, but some days, you wish you could believe in an easier, maybe even happier someday. The guilt that comes with that yearning is as

MISSING FROM YOU

The loneliness in widowhood is palpable, particularly at the beginning of the journey. The missing presence of your beloved by your side is something that follows you everywhere you go. You literally feel the emptiness of him missing from you in your body, the ache of aloneness following along beside you like a shadow. There are days your mind tricks you and your heart beats with delight as the phone rings, momentarily forgetting it can't be him on the other end. Making meals for one throbs with loneliness. The master bedroom in most homes is designed for two, an inherent reminder of your oneness. Crawling into a bed with space for two stabs like a knife some nights. Looking into a closet with half the space empty was too much for Suzanne, so she shopped to fill up the void with enough clothes for two.

While I fully honor the lived desperation and longing that is felt in your body with every step in grief, I know there's more to it than missing him. We make our loneliness mean something about us. In our aloneness, we find ourselves believing we are unsafe, unloved, and unworthy too. Not only that, but we're so sure it will be this way forever now that he's gone. This is where your healing work begins. When we come toward ourselves in loneliness, we find our most powerful companion within.

ONE PLEASE

Just me please. No, I'm not waiting for anyone. Oh, the words you must say aloud when you take yourself for a date. The hostess is often unconcerned about hiding her raised eyebrow as she seats you alone. It's fascinating that in the year 2017, whether widowed, divorced, or happily married, women still feel like a social anomaly to be alone in public. And yet, walking boldly into the social world alone when the time feels right is an empowering path to overcoming the pain we associate with aloneness in grief.

Pam told me about the first wedding she attended after her husband died. *The invitation was addressed just to me, no plus one. Apparently they had decided it was too soon after his death to offer me the option of bringing a date. I didn't have a date I wanted to bring, but it felt judgmental all the same. I felt so alone at a ceremony celebrating the love of my dear friends, surrounded by couples dancing the night away in the name of love. Every other place setting was a set of keys tied together with the couples names attached. Mine was one key. One name. I felt insane for being so triggered by the nametag at a table, but I was.*

Pam wasn't telling me anything I hadn't heard before. Together, we walked further down the path of self-love and explored it from a lens of loneliness. She lamented to me: *Loneliness means there is no one to count on but myself. That's scary, but what's even worse is loneliness means no one chooses me. No one loves me. No one has my back. There's no one to tell me I'm beautiful or snuggle into at the end of the day. I'm alone and it feels like I don't fit anywhere when it's just me.*

Slowly, we leaned into each of those stories that felt very real and deeply painful. Slowly and carefully, we practiced replacing those spiraling beliefs with something that was truer. Without forcing it to override what she was feeling, Pam learned to remind herself: *I can be alone and not be lonely.*

It can be a wild and sometimes wicked journey to truly internalize this truth. It's also a journey that's worth the taking as you find yourself so much freer on the other side of this deeply healing ride. It's a delicious feeling to have arrived at the place where you're one of your favorite companions and aloneness no longer feels like a dagger in your belly. From this space, you can acknowledge there once was a time of deep hurt in aloneness, but no longer. This doesn't mean you don't choose company, it simply means that even when you're alone with yourself in the world, you feel safe, worthy and loved.

HAPPINESS IS AN INSIDE JOB

Love is rad, no doubt. So many of us and those who worry about us in life after loss hope and pray and wish for love to swoop in and save us from the nightmare that is being a widow. It's lonely there in widow land. And yet, *Loneliness is a sign you are in desperate need of yourself,* Rumi said. After her husband died, Maggie didn't understand what it was to love herself. She wanted other people to do it for her, and genuinely didn't understand how to proceed when all the teachers and gurus kept blabbing on about this "self-love" stuff that felt like BS. It made her throw grown-up temper tantrums about *why was it so hard?!*

Maggie and I worked together to bring her pain and resistance crumbling down around her so she could open to the reality of love. It happened with powerful tenderness *from* Maggie, *for* Maggie. I said very matter-of-factly to her during one of our calls: *Have a tantrum. Stomp your feet. Cry as much as you need to and make it ugly. But no one is coming to save you. No one will EVER be able to do this for you. Only you can love yourself the way you're craving.* What Maggie had to learn was to fill in the gaping loneliness with her own love. Without it, no one else's love would be adequate to fill the void. And she did. Months later, she was literally a whole new woman with a new lens on life. Maggie finally found enough love for herself to feel whole.

REFLECTION

To master your reality, you must first master your thoughts and identify your limiting beliefs. Can you identify a thought pattern that plays out in your mind? Are there beliefs that feel absolutely true and cause you so much pain? These are the places where we can use awareness and inquiry to understand and release the self-imposed limits that feel binding. Free write what feels most true for you right now as you complete the prompts below:

- *I struggle to accept...*
- *Closure will look like...*
- *When I feel lonely, I...*

Chapter Eight

Healing Made Tangible

When you feel as though your mind, body, and life have been hijacked by a nightmare that won't end in grief, you can choose to practice coming home to yourself and a more grounded reality through ritual. That word often carries some serious implications about religion, and may even evoke fear and shame for some. Upon further inquiry, we come to see there is ritual in our most honored cultural traditions.

So many of us don't know the history and meaning of these things we assign less powerful words like *tradition* or *nostalgia* to, but rituals they remain. Without batting an eye, we move the tassel on the graduation cap, and raise our right hand while taking an oath. In a wedding day ritual, we place a ring on the left ring finger of our beloved. In our widowhood, we came face to face with the sacred meaning that ring on our finger carried as we grappled with performing the ritual of removing it, too. Without giving it a second thought, we light candles as we whisper prayers, hoist glasses of champagne high while offering a toast to mark the most special occasions, and smile when we hear bells ringing through town on Sunday morning.

WHAT IS RITUAL?

Modern ritual doesn't necessarily involve blood sacrifice, and that's certainly not what we're exploring here. Wikipedia defines ritual as "a sequence of activities involving gestures, words, and objects, performed in a sequestered place, and performed according to a set sequence." Ritual is about doing something with intention to signify the shift from daily life into sacred. At its most basic, ritual is the way we create space to notice what we notice, deeply feel, and acknowledge a profound experience or rite of passage, whether positive or negative.

RITUAL ISN'T A QUICK FIX

It's worth noting there's no way to force yourself above the pain of grief with any of these practices. If there's any grasping or forcing in the energy you're bringing into this work, you're not going anywhere. When we cling to these practices to save us or skip over the painful work of traveling through the shadow side of human emotions, it's called "spiritual bypass."

Bypass behaves a little like the silver linings you hear people talk about and a lot like faking it 'til you make it. It's putting on a happy face when you're dying inside. None of us get to skip the pain and the work of grief. None of us has to stay inside that place of suffering forever either. We're not trying to escape the pain, we need it all so we can process the unthinkable shift in our reality. Ritual helps us touch and hold pieces of the heart process that is otherwise so internalized and invisible.

Ritual is about embodied authenticity. Often a ritual will push you into a place of deeper felt discomfort before arriving in peace on the other side. You can literally feel the shift in perspective when it comes. You can feel ritual allowing deeply buried emotions to finally pass safely through and be expressed. In the practice of ritual, you are able to literally rewire your neuropathways, inviting profound change. When you do this work, the suffering subsides to reveal what's truly there and the path to healing is yours. Even inside the space of ritual, vulnerability and truth must be at the forefront. Bring your whole heart to the practices and leave behind expectations and meaning-making. What you'll find there will be profound and life changing.

SACRED WITNESS

These practices will often feel more profound when your pain is most acute. Knowing what to choose and when with these practices comes back to noticing what you notice once again. Everything we explored in the previous chapter about the limiting beliefs, thoughts, and fears of your mind will come into play as you cultivate the witnessing mind, as Yoganand Michael Carroll called it. This is purely the ability to experience fears, beliefs and emotions that are uncomfortable, even painful, allow them to exist and not assign them meaning that becomes suffering.

The witnessing mind is about cultivating awareness of what you're feeling and not needing to push it away. *I am aware that I am angry right now.* You take no action unless there is true danger, you just notice. There's nothing to do but feel the anger and inquire more deeply about the anger. Often, the anger is coming from a perceived threat that activates your already stressed survival center in grief to demand an immediate and heightened response. The witnessing mind is not about inaction; it's about intentional action. It's about noticing what you notice, allowing it to be there, inquiring more deeply about what you truly need instead of allowing the fight or flight response to take over. It's acting and choosing consciously when the time is right.

TELL YOUR STORY

Jasmine casually mentioned to the grocery store cashier that she was happy to be finally finding her way around the grocery store after her recent move. The cashier smiled and asked where she had moved from, then further inquired if she had moved because of her husband's job. *I was just getting out my credit card as she asked the question. I got tunnel vision and felt all panicky. Right there in the middle of the grocery story I had to say out loud that we moved because my husband died.*

I don't know if it was worse having to tell my story to a stranger in the grocery check out lane or bracing for the pity, hushed and hurried condolence being muttered and look of shock on that poor cashier's face. I find myself bracing for the question

I can literally HEAR coming in those seemingly superficial conversations like a freight train coming down the tracks, horn blaring. Some days I end up having to go through this process two or three times, Jasmine told me. *I hate having to tell my story everywhere I go and facing the pity response. I hate watching people scuttle away from me as fast as they can when they hear what happened.* Jasmine is one of many who has shared this exhausting experience, longing to be free from the pain and shame she feels each time.

After working together around her beliefs and perceptions, Jasmine now uses her storytelling as a healing ritual. She started by writing it down. *All the details went into my journal,* Jasmine told me. *I wrote it more than once. Sometimes it came out sad. Sometimes it came out mad. Sometimes I ended up writing about our love story more than his death. Every time I wrote it, I felt more and more release. I tell the story of my husband's death differently now,* Jasmine said. *I tell people unapologetically and without hesitation. I let tears come if they do and dry eyes remain when they don't and I don't feel bad about either option.*

I hold space for their awkward reactions, but I don't make it mean anything about me and my story. I give them permission to be shocked, to feel pity, to be unsure about what to say next. I reassure them with my humanness and vulnerability. I thank them for listening. Every time I say my story out loud and look another human in the eyes as I do so, I can feel it becoming more true, more mine, and less triggering. I can feel myself being freed from the need to protect their experience with it. I actually feel the healing wrapping around me as I claim the story and help them hear what I need them to about how to be with me.

Every time you connect with and own this piece of your story, it takes you one step further into the new story, the one where it's just you and who you're becoming. The love story you shared is part of you. His death is part of you. Everything that will happen in your life after loss is part of your story. It sometimes feels like torture but choosing to reclaim it let's you take back the power from your pain. It's all healing.

MAKING IT TANGIBLE

Just as storytelling can bring about deep processing and release the pain, so too can ritual. In this case, ritual becomes simply the act of grieving in a way you can see, touch, taste, feel and hear. Writing him letters can become a ritual. You can take it even further by going to the same special space, lighting a candle, and maybe even burning those letters to ashes to be carried to him on the wind. Even doing your taxes can become a ritual, writing *deceased* over and over and over. In doing so, your hand is physically honoring the reality of his death and expressing it repeatedly. It becomes more real, no longer a thing to plead with, as you do so. It doesn't mean you're glad it happened, it just means you are becoming free from pain as you acknowledge your reality in as many ways as it takes to makes sense of.

Ritual becomes the act of interacting with your physical home space. Touch it all: his shirts, his shoes, his worn leather belt, his toiletry bag. Notice what gives you chill bumps. Notice what brings you to tears. Notice what feels like "just things". Notice what about your physical space hurts. Is it those boxes of his you step over every time you come home?

Move them; not to avoid seeing them but to touch the boxes that *feel* like they have the power to make you feel pain. Touch them, push them, carry them to wherever they need to go that feels like peace. Maybe it's to the corner of the garage. Maybe it's to donation. Maybe it's to storage until a day when you're ready to face them again.

Is it his unfinished DIY project in the back yard? Ask or hire someone with the right skills to help you finish it. Choose action that feels like empowerment. Choose permission to tend to these pieces of your space, even if you know it will come with some pain before the peace it will bring. Notice what feels important. Notice what feels like closeness to him. Notice the parts of your home and physical things that elicit peace and connection to him. Let go of the expectation that you should put it away. Choose permission to keep what feels like salve on the wound and eliminate what feels like a plague of prolonged pain in your space. Touch the things that feel like pain and take empowered action to interface with them. You get to decide what they mean, the power they hold over you, and what becomes of them.

HOW CAN I LOVE YOU TODAY?

Remember the way Maggie shared her frustration-turned-tantrum about figuring out how to get to the roots of self-love? That same day, I shared a practice I had received from a healer years before that was life changing. Self-love is often so intangible. It's a pretty-sounding, elusive concept that so few of us understand *how* to do. This self-love practice I offered Maggie allowed her to soften beyond the resistance and into healing yet another jagged edge of her broken heart. It helped deeply with my own healing too.

You begin simply by looking at yourself in the mirror. Don't look at the stuff the world tells you is wrong with your body or your skin. Look to see you. Really look *into* you. Look into your eyes to see your soul the way a lover would look at you. Every day, as many times a day as it takes, look into the mirror, look into the depths of your own eyes, as far down into your soul as feels safe to see. Look there and just notice. And when you feel ready, whisper if you must, just this question: *How can I love you today?* Whisper it *to yourself*. Keep looking and listen. Listen.

Don't force an answer, wait for the truth to bubble up and don't make wrong whatever it is you hear. Hear the answer like a beloved would hear you and hold what you heard tenderly. You're learning self love. Show up day after day, no matter how awkward and fake and scary it feels at first. Keep not believing in it for a while if it feels better and do it anyway. Every time, keep noticing how doing this simple practice of looking into your own eyes and inquiring stirs something in you so foreign and yet so alive that you can't help but continue the mirror practice.

This tiny beginning becomes a never-ending tunnel of exploring what it is to love yourself. In time, you won't need to see into your eyes in the mirror. You'll be able to reach deep into your soul on the days when life feels hardest and simply inquire, *how can I love you today?* The answers will help guide your way. The answers will remind you when you understand what pieces of the chrysalis you're still constructing. The answers will help you ask for the right kind of support. The answers will allow you to choose a life that feels like yours to live. You will continually be excavating who is in there, some of your most rad and sometimes ragged pieces buried so deep. Each time you turn inward, you'll keep holding tenderly whatever it is you find, and learning what it is to come home to you. Slowly you will come to believe you are loved wholly and you are more powerful than you know.

LOVING KINDNESS

It seems counterintuitive yet almost universal that at some point in our journey into grief, we widows end up punishing ourselves so intensely. Maya Rachel Stein, wrote in her poem *The Beauty of Grief*, "… No one knows how harshly she spoke to herself, flagellated her already fragile spirit, lay on her bed with her forearms pinching her eyelids flat, and made mad proclamations against her weak, fractured heart. No one knows the hours she's devoted to circling her sadness like a vulture, the mileage she's worn into her soles, walking the hills of her city in a series of unsuccessful attempts at forgetting." Anyone who's ever loved and lost can relate to this anger directed inward. We feel angry and shame ourselves equally for our ability to feel so painfully deep and for our inability to stop feeling the deep ache of grief, always asking *what's wrong with me?* In these moments, above all, I invite you to connect with a loving kindness mantra gifted to me by my life coach Mindy early in the process of creating my own chrysalis.

You can practice this loving kindness ritual anywhere at any time. It's so discreet, only you will know it's taking place. You connect your thoughts with a safe, calming physical touch to provide them an anchor to be grounded to. When you find your thoughts to be punishing, criticizing, demeaning, or belittling yourself, put your hand on your wrist. This gentle self-touch on or near your pulse point is the first piece of this ritual; a gesture of bringing intentional loving awareness to your experience and yourself. The touch is tender, the same way you'd hold close a small child needing comfort. The touch simply says without words, *I see you. I value you. You are safe.*

As you touch your wrist, you turn your awareness to your breath, for a few moments inhaling and exhaling more slowly and deeply than you normally would. As you feel your shoulders soften with your breath, you turn your attention to any areas in your body where you might be carrying tension in this moment of activated stress response. With that same tenderness, as you notice those areas of tension, you envision sending the deep calming breaths you're taking to soften those places. Once you've felt your physical body soften, you bring your awareness to any emotions you might be holding as you continue to breathe deeply. See if you can move toward your difficult emotions with that tenderness. Instead of rejecting it, simply notice that it's there and envision the calming breaths wrapping around even those emotions. When you've moved through each component of this loving kindness ritual involving breath, body, and emotions, you close it with spoken or silently thought words of kindness toward yourself. A loving kindness mantra: *May I be safe. May I be peaceful. May I be kind to myself. May I accept myself exactly as I am.*

ON MANTRA

We've all seen or heard the chanting of monks, whether in person or on TV. Often we relate mantra to what we've heard them doing: making sounds or words that we don't understand in a deeply religious show of devotion to some deity or another. Sometimes we make fun of it. Sometimes it seems a little crazy. I'm inviting you to explore mantra in a way that has nothing to do with religion and everything to do with coming home to yourself.

Mantra is about raising awareness, bringing you present, and moving powerful energy through you. Mantra is about shifting out of limiting beliefs into peace. Just as in ritual, mantra must be entered into with deep vulnerability, openness, and free from expectation. If you choose mantra and demand it to save you, you'll never experience the bliss it can offer. Practice mantra humbly as a form of self-love and healing, and so it will be.

Mantra is a lifeline when the pain begins to spiral, bringing you back to something more true than the stories your survival center loves to spin out of control. Gently repeating phrases like *I am the foundation of my life* lets you reclaim your inherent worth, power, and potential. Repeating the mantra *I graciously accept and fearlessly activate my power and strength* allows you to call upon yourself when the pain threatens to carry you away.

TURNING TO MANTRA

Leann was a client who was responding to life with intense reactivity in the aftermath of her husband's death. *I'm horrified watching myself lashing out, super defensive. I'm responding like everyone is attacking me when most of it I can rationally see is just day-to-day things. Nothing has changed except my tolerance for it all and my anxiety. I feel like I have to protect myself from everyone now. There is so much urgency; I'm reacting before I even have time to think. Every conversation comes out more powerful than it needs to. I'm reactive to everything. I hate who I'm becoming,* Leann told me.

Because of her ability to notice what she was noticing about her own reactivity (and not liking it), we were able to get more clear on what was happening. Together we created a mantra she could use when she felt triggered to reactivity. Creating your own mantra acts as an emergency response system, in the same way we're trained to respond to dangerous disasters like catching fires and earthquakes with an engrained response that becomes instinctive. *Stop, drop and roll. Seek shelter immediately.* Creating your own mantra can replace triggered reactivity with instinctive, intentional peace; a place you can come back to when the storm of life feels too big.

CORD CUTTING

The first time I heard Elizabeth DiAlto describe a cord cutting ritual on her "Untame the Wild Soul" podcast, I have to admit I laughed out loud a little to envision it. I've since come to own it as a powerful energy-shifting ritual that's accessible and quick for anyone to implement. The gist of the cord cutting ritual is this: identify any experience, conversation, thought that feels energetically bad and "cut" the energetic cords between you and it. It looks as simple as karate chopping the air in front of you with both hands. You can simply make it an intentionally physical act of separating yourself from the bad experience, like animals who intentionally shake themselves out of a fight or flight response after a trauma. You can also make it mean something deeper.

In an energetic sense, you are literally severing the energetic cords that invisibly but undoubtedly exist between you and the negative encounter. It's simply holding firm the energetic boundaries of anything you are unwilling to take on. Madame DiAlto says she cuts cords to "anything that's not mine," as in negative encounters or projections that make her feel shame, guilt, fear or just extra small. In grief, it's easy to begin feeling the energy of those around us. As we feel ourselves coming unraveled, we often turn to our people for guidance on what's real and what they think we're "allowed" to feel. Every widow I've ever spoken to has shared her experiences of people projecting their fear, pain, grief, shame, and pity onto them. It's exhausting to take on other's projections of what they believe our experience to be. When you start feeling negative thoughts, beliefs, or energies, turn to a simple cord cutting ritual and watch the energetic shift happen.

CULTIVATING GRATITUDE

A gratitude practice is simply acknowledging and expressing gratitude and cultivating the ability and desire to look for it in the first place. This too can become ritual. It takes a "grateful" feeling and integrates it further but expressing it in written or spoken words, allowing you to further internalize the experience that is so vital when most of your energy and thoughts revolve around the pain of grief. It might look like keeping a small journal with you to make notes when you notice an encounter with gratitude, no matter how small. It might look like making a list at the end of the day, reflecting on each piece of the day and noting what you were grateful for. Some days, my gratitude was for something as simple as an uninterrupted shower. Other days it was gratitude for dry shampoo that allowed me not to *look* like I had missed a shower for a third day in a row.

It might look like finding an accountability partner and calling each other once a week to take a walk together and talk gratitude. That sounds like something to be grateful for! It might be enough to simply notice, pause, smile, and continue on with your day. Whatever it looks like for you, what's important here is that cultivating the awareness to look for and notice the brief bits of gratitude you experience in life shifts your psychic disposition in a profound way. From inside grief, it's easy to get trapped in victim mentality and the language of suffering. From inside grief, cultivating a gratitude practice begins to break those patterns and facilitate more ease in bringing you to the present moment in life. There is healing in seeing the gratitude for what's right in front of you, no matter how small it may seem. It doesn't override what's missing from you, but it shifts your awareness and energy in the powerful direction of healing. Your physiology responds to a gratitude practice. It's widely documented in academia that gratitude actually improves physical health and mental health. Slowly, through the ritual of gratitude, you not only retrain your thoughts toward presence and peace, but you alleviate physical symptoms common in grief like sleeplessness, high blood pressure, and anxiety too.

I realize from inside grief, there can be a deep need and desire to resist anything that smells like gratitude or peace. Without forcing it, lean in and ask yourself why gratitude feels so terrifying. No matter how desperate life gets, it's there in the most mundane if you're willing to see it. For so long, my gratitude was the one thing to carry me through the emptiness of my life deep inside my grief. This gratitude practice is really about cultivating awareness. It's paying attention to the things that look beautiful and feel comforting (no matter how superficial they might be).

MAYAN GRIEF AS PRAISE

Two months after my husband died, I heard Mayan Shaman Martín Prechtel speak about grief as a form of praise. He says those of us who "cannot weep properly, where you look bad when you're done, when your hair is missing, and your clothes are ripped and you're down in the street," also do not understand praise. Prechtel paints a picture of grief as the highest form of praise because it means simply that "you miss what you have lost." His culturally informed perspective on grieving was one of few that truly resonated with me and began a shift in the way I allowed my grief to express. Alongside a gratitude practice in your life after loss, you can express gratitude for the journey that happened before his death too. Instead of seeing the pain of my grief as a thing I was forced to endure, I came to experience it as a deeply felt expression of gratitude for what had been mine.

UNTAME YOURSELF 2, 3, 4 PRACTICE

One particular gratitude ritual that is full of impact and easy to integrate into your morning is the "2, 3, 4 practice," outlined in Elizabeth DiAlto's book *Untame Yourself: Reconnect to the Lost Art, Power, and Freedom of Being a Woman*. She lays out a simple framework for beginning your day present, connected to your body, and grateful in just nine minutes. For two minutes you sit still and breathe. For three minutes, you move your body slowly in any way that feels good without overthinking it or giving it a rigid structure (think sensual slow dance). For four minutes, you grab a journal and your favorite pen and write without filtering about "what's good and what [you] want." Anything goes. Without needing to muscle your way through an overwhelming sequence full of unfamiliar language, this 2-3-4 practice once again makes you the guru and brings you home to what's actually true. It frees you from swirling stories and limiting beliefs, guiding yourself back to presence and gratitude. From that centered and grounded place of peace, you begin your day.

A SPACE TO REMEMBER

Ritual can also take the form of creating an altar or special space in your home, a visual place to pass by throughout the day, bringing intention to the remembering. It is a place to go to when you long to connect. Feel free to separate from any religious connotation or expectation that word might carry for you. In its purest form, a remembrance altar is a physical, tangible, space to express both grief and gratitude for the beloved you've buried. It looks like flowers on the roadside and candles lit in the aftermath of terrorism and natural disaster alike. Made more personal, it can simply be a table in your home adorned with items that elicit a connection to your deceased beloved, perhaps a beautiful picture and small stones and trinkets that were special to your story. It can be decorated with flowers and include candles to be used in a variety of ways. It can become the place you use to communicate with him in the beyond, whether out loud or in written form. It can be a place you record your gratitude for the memories or the aches of your heart you're longing to heal. There is no right way to make an altar except to make it yours. If it elicits peace, gratitude and tender connection, you're on the right track.

RETRIGGERED

When we've experienced the trauma of burying our husband, it can be common to be powerfully triggered when you learn of the death of someone else's spouse. Sometimes this shows up as powerful empathy. You have the superpower of truly understanding a piece of their pain in ways no one else can. This makes you an invaluable ally as they begin their journey into grief. If this is what you're experiencing, I encourage you to go toward them with an open heart and no expectation of being needed. Sometimes it's as simple as letting them know you understand and you're available if and when they want to connect. However, sometimes the death of someone else's spouse can activate you to a trauma state and your survival center becomes highly sensitized, as though the trauma feels like it's happening to you all over again.

RELIVING TRAUMA

Melissa's husband died in a military accident years ago, but when she heard about an eerily similar story that happened to a friend of a friend she had never met, she came undone. She became a nervous wreck. She couldn't sleep and was quick to tears. She was terrified to answer the phone and kept watching the front steps to her house for unexpected visitors. While she had long since felt as though she had moved through her grief to a place of living, this recent death of the spouse of someone she didn't know reactivated her own trauma.

In our work together, she came to understand that she was literally re-experiencing the trauma of being notified of his death. She felt herself waiting for those military officers to arrive at her door and tell her that her husband had been killed in action. Again. On a rational level, she knew it was impossible but her every thought, gasping breath, and the quickened pace of her heart told her otherwise. There exists in grief a form of PTSD, particularly in cases of sudden bereavement. Your ability to notice what you notice (that you're suddenly fearing your trauma might happen to you all over again) can allow you to access ritual and mantra to help you ground those spiraling thoughts. The mantra becomes something like: *The trauma and grief happened. It is over. I am safe.* This is also a time to employ discernment. If the reactivated trauma becomes debilitating, never hesitate to connect with a professional support practitioner to find your way through this potentially intense reactivated trauma state safely and completely.

REFLECTION

While so much of our journey through grief is learning to tend to our inner world of our thoughts and beliefs, ritual helps us process this work a bit more *out loud*, expressed in a way that our five senses can access. Consider what things you have done or considered doing that were simply ritual: laying flowers graveside, leaving coins on headstones, lighting candles, and saying prayers are all forms of ritual. What has ritual helped you access, feel, process, or tap into? Free write what feels most true for you right now as you complete the prompts below:

- *Some rituals I've participated in without realizing it are...*
- *The ritual I feel most compelled to try is...*
- *I am willing to step out of my comfort zone in the name of healing and...*

Chapter Nine

Body Wisdom

T aking the grief made tangible practices even further, we now turn to your body as a mechanism for healing and a tool to inform the path ahead in life after loss. Learning to sense and read your body's signals is learning to understand the nonverbal language your most authentic, inner Self is constantly communicating. When you learn to connect with the signals of your body, there comes to be deep knowing and clarity at every turn.

The body offers a very clear feedback mechanism if you're willing to learn it. Unfortunately, we have all too often vilified our bodies and as a result, we've learned to operate in and trust in our heads exclusively. The problem is, as Rachel Maddox explains, "when the brain is stuck in a trauma spell—meaning the reptilian part is hyper activated, and the higher-level parts are less accessible—it feels almost like having a slight brain injury to your innate brilliance...your brain has been hijacked by trauma." As a result, it becomes increasingly easy to get caught in a negative feedback loop of limiting beliefs and spiraling thoughts we explored in earlier chapters. Your body is here to guide you from the depths of your *essential self* when your rational mind cannot be relied on to help you find your way. In tapping into your body for wisdom, the journey through grief is even easier to navigate when the knowing and clarity becomes strong.

HEARING THE BODY'S WISDOM

Learning to understand your body's signals is as simple as intentionally noticing what you notice about the way your body feels and *when* it feels that way. To understand what's being communicated through sensory perception, we must, as life coach Martha Beck describes it, "calibrate" our body compass. It's simply learning to listen to and understand what's being communicated by an embodied language that is felt rather than spoken. It is here that we access deep clarity and knowing.

There's a brief exercise that involves bringing your body to complete stillness and as present as possible, similar to the loving kindness practice introduced earlier. You then envision a linear scale with zero at the middle. At the far left of the zero (where a math minded person might write a -10), you draw a sad face indicating this end of the spectrum is a *big bad yuck* life experience. At the opposite end of the line (where the +10 would go), you envision a happy face indicating this side of the line is a joyful, juicy life experience. Using this as reference, the first step of learning to identify and understand your body feedback is to fine tune what each end of the spectrum really feels like in your body. To begin, select a memory in your life (preferably not a deeply traumatic one) that felt like a "big bad yuck" (or -10 rated) experience; just about the worst you could feel. Don't overthink it, just notice what memory immediately pops through. If you don't filter things out, you'll come up with something fairly easily. You then take a few moments to remember as many details as possible about that experience.

Once you've really connected with the details of that painful memory, you pan back from the specifics just enough to notice what you're physically feeling in your body while still mentally inside that memory. You're looking for things felt physically, not emotions or thoughts. Things like: *my shoulders are heavy and tightening or my toes are all curling up and I'm tensing my calves.* Start at your feet and systematically bring your awareness little by little up your body, noting every tiny detail along the way. *There's a tightening behind my shoulder blades. I've got a headache at the back of my head I recognize.* You'll be surprised how much you're able to notice that likely you haven't paid much heed to before. When you're done, try to write it all down for later reference. This is indicative of how your body communicates with you when you're having or thinking about having a *big bad yuck* experience. You've dialed in the physical ways your body communicates to you when something feels "bad".

To continue the lesson in your body's sensory language, you repeat the exact same steps on a remembered experience that registers as neither good nor bad to identify your *mundane, no big deal* (neutral) feeling state. After recalling all the details of a boring, day-to-day life kind of thing that lands on or around the zero mark of your experience spectrum, you'll notice what you're feeling in your body. Really spend some time on it and scan from bottom to top. There may not be a lot to note at the neutral feeling state because, well, it's neutral. Once you've made note of what shows up in your body when you're experiencing a neutral event or emotional state, you repeat the process again with a positive feeling memory. This will help you learn to feel and understand how a positive feeling experience (+10 on the spectrum) shows up in your body.

Like many deeply exploratory practices, learning to experience your body's communication process is a practice that may not make sense right away. It takes time to learn how to listen to what our body is saying. Like most new things, it's much easier when facilitated by a coach. As with every practice we've explored, the body language decoding requires you to consciously step back from your rational mind that is constantly searching for the "right" answers and consistently casts judgment on the real answers. Hearing the body requires feeling.

THE BODY TALKS

Once you've learned to understand how your body responds physically in the icky, neutral, and fabulous experiences, you've got data to work with. Taking what you've learned, you return once more to the practice of noticing what you notice, this time about how you feel in your body. Now that you've got these indicators and measurements provided by the skin you're in and sourced from truest Self, you can use what you've learned to help you choose what's most true for you in any situation you'll face in life after loss. This information helps us determine what we truly need so we can ask for it instead of accepting what we think we're allowed. This information shows us when we need to finally choose self-care or establish some boundaries where we've previously been slugging away in the martyr kingdom of living from our *shoulds*. This information helps us override the voice of *the Curator*, directing us to operate from self-preservation and avoidance of pain. This information helps us trust our intuition when we're faced with any decision, big or small when we remember to tune in.

Instead of stewing for days and going to every guru on the east side of town and booking an emergency session with your therapist, you come fully present and consider that situation and all the possible options with your embodied wisdom and felt communication in mind. You notice what you notice about how your body feels when you consider choosing option A versus option B. *If I envision choosing option A, what do I notice about how I feel in my body? If I consider the implications of choosing option B, what shifts in my body?* Almost every time, one path will feel light and open and one will feel heavy and achy. When that happens, your *innermost Self* via the body has spoken. Your body can help you identify the most true-for-you path to peace. You don't need to reconsider it from what you *think* you *should* do or what others expect from you. You lean in and listen to the body wisdom being clearly communicated. The answers you find there are unbelievably clear. This practice makes accessible such deep knowing and clarity in the journey of life after loss.

MAINTAINING THE MACHINE

As powerful as the body's clear feedback is, it requires essential and preventative maintenance to ensure its continued health and wholeness. Science reveals more and more clearly every day the undeniable connection between the mind and body. For so long (at least in recent history), we've considered them as separate entities. Finally, we're coming back around to what ancient cultures worldwide have recognized far beyond the measuring capacity of modern science. The mind and the body are one system informing and affecting one another profoundly.

We typically evaluate, measure, and study only the emotional and psychological impacts of a lived traumatic experience and so often miss the deep implications of trauma held and manifested in the physical body. Beyond the painful emotions and limiting beliefs that result from trauma and intense grief, the body holds that trauma for us at the cellular level too. Thankfully, there are plentiful healing modalities available to access deep healing within the physical body. When we choose practitioners who help us move through and release embodied trauma, deep healing is felt in the mind, heart, and soul too.

EXERCISE AND MOVEMENT

We've all heard exercise is an unbeatable tool to mitigate the potential for depression, among other health challenges we're facing at an epidemic rate. We've heard the advice to exercise away our pain and depression, and it's been documented to be useful by solid science. Exercise and movement can absolutely be a powerful healing tool, but it can also deeply hinder the important healing work happening in grief too. Without careful awareness, exercise can become a distraction from our healing process. Without conscious consideration, exercise can become an obsession. There are times exercise in extremes can feel more like punishment, self-loathing, and a new list of *shoulds* to fail at.

Sometimes exercise can even take the form of identity in life after loss.

When we're deep in grief, choosing intensely demanding exercise can often require an override of the softening and stillness we're cultivating as we make space for the chrysalis that is the basis of our healing. As with every other offering found in this book, I encourage you to notice what you notice about the exercise you're choosing. If it makes you feel powerfully alive, strong, and lit up inside, your body will tell you to keep doing what you're doing. If, however, you find yourself more exhausted and having to shame yourself into participating, your body communication will likely be sending you a clear message to change course. It's not that you have to give up on exercise. It's simply that there may be a type of body movement that is most aligned with the physical output your trauma-activated physiology is capable of handling at the moment. Notice what you notice and soften to meet your body where it is.

JUST BREATHE

While it's not an exercise, breathwork (or *pranayama* as yogis call it) is the most profound embodiment exercise that provides a deep level of healing to the mind-body complex. Richard Faulds explains in *Kripalu Yoga,* "It seems counterintuitive that anyone would need to learn to do something as natural as breathing freely and deeply. Why do we restrict our breathing? One answer is that tightening the belly muscles is a natural short-term response to stress that dulls our ability to feel and protects us physically and emotionally. If this response becomes habitual, it creates a host of undesirable consequences. Through the practice of being present and breath awareness, [it] returns us to full feeling and releases chronic muscular and emotional tension."

As described in the loving kindness practice introduced earlier in the book, this can be as simple as sitting still and breathing slowly with intention. There are more in-depth breath practices that a yoga teacher or holistic practitioner can teach you, but a very profound and accessible place to start is learning simply to breathe slowly with intention. The shift in your mental clarity and general sensations in your neutral feeling body communication will be astonishing. Simply put, a regular pranayama practice feels like bliss and relief.

BODYWORK

Shaman Martín Prechtel shares the Mayan perspective of unexpressed grief becoming "crystalized tears held within the body," We know now there's science to back up the physical manifestations of the traumas of our lives, such as chronic pain, chronic sleep issues, inflammation in the body, chronic gastro-intestinal issues, chronic headaches, lethargy, brain fog and more. What practitioners of various holistic healing modalities understand is the nuance of complex intricacies within the whole self like fascia, energy, and how to facilitate movement and release of these trapped traumas in our physical body to cultivate both physical wellness and wholeness as a person with mind, body, and spirit.

Based on my own personal healing journey and what I've experienced supporting others as a certified yoga instructor and Reiki practitioner, I deeply believe bodywork is at the forefront of creating a sacred and meaningful chrysalis and profound space for deep healing. Bodywork is an essential foundation for all other healing work. We continue to explore the measurable science to back up the fact that trauma actually shows up in our physical bodies and can be released through bodywork and other holistic healing modalities. It's a beautiful thing when modern science finally begins to scratch the surface of understanding ancient holistic healing modalities.

Bodywork is a process that facilitates a deep release and healing experience.

Different than "massage," a bodywork professional brings a deeper understanding of the intricacies and interconnectedness of mind, body and spirit to their work. They are typically trained in multiple non-Western healing modalities that can be intuitively applied interchangeably, based on what is being symptomatically presented in the physical body and related mental and emotional circumstances. So much of what we call massage in spa-like settings dabbles at the most superficial edge of bodywork, often a relaxing experience where a masseuse systematically rubs oil into your skin. Bodywork is a more profound energetic and physical healing experience.

Just like all services providers, there comes a wide array of what's possible in the realm of healing work in the body and you must choose your provider carefully. Often referred to as holistic practitioners or lightworkers, these bodywork practitioners understand the deeply tied connections between mind, body, and spirit and are interfacing with them all within the scope of their healing work. Make no mistake, their work will be experienced on a physical level as a deeply relaxing massage or other physical services like Reiki, therapeutic yoga, acupuncture, or chiropractic care. Its healing potential will go far beyond a relaxing hour spent in a candlelit room. Profound healing and release occurs at the cellular level when bodywork becomes a regular part of your chrysalis and self-care, creating space for the wholeness of Self in mind, body, and spirit on this journey in life after loss.

ANXIETY EMBODIED

Sensory overwhelm. Thyroid and hormone imbalance. Inflammation. Adrenal fatigue. Reactivity. Anger. Exhaustion. Lethargy. Anxiety. Exhaustion, exhaustion, exhaustion. These are all "symptoms" of grief that have more to do with our trauma than a separate, treatable sickness. There's not a widow I have spoken to who hasn't shared an ongoing, frustrating battle with some or all of the physical manifestations of grief and trauma above and more. As we explored earlier, the physiology of an activated trauma has immediate and intense ramifications on the body. Science acknowledges the unexplored rift in modern trauma resolution therapies that separate the mind from the physical symptoms exhibited in the body. We're treating the body separately from the treatments and therapies being applied to the mind.

What we're only starting to understand is the long-term physical ailments associated with unresolved trauma and grief that often outlast the consciously felt emotional impacts of the same. As I said about the chrysalis, the physical needs of the body must be prioritized to allow the heart and soul to experience relief and healing too. In tending to the deep care of our bodies in the form of primarily non-Western bodywork modalities, we're creating a healthy physical container for the head, heart, and soul-level healing work we're doing too. It's not about medicating away symptoms, it's about supporting the physical body as it allows the embodied trauma to move through and slowly release along with support being applied to the processing in head and heart.

YOGA

Yogi Amrit Desai wrote, "Yesterday is dead. Tomorrow isn't born. We can only live in the present." While most equate the practice of yoga with cute spandex pants and a physical challenge that helps us stay fit and alleviate stress, there's so much more to it. Yoga allows us to "be fully present in the moment-by-moment experience of being alive," Richard Faulds wrote in his book *Kripalu Yoga*. There is no better way to stay fully present and embodied and therefore in awareness of your body communication and the needs of your physical machine than a regular yoga practice. Yoga syncs your body and your breath. Yoga allows you to regularly cultivate the witnessing mind that allows you to notice and explore your limiting beliefs and activated survival responses and choose differently. Yoga allows you to move energy through the body, without which residual trauma can become manifest as physical ailments and sickness. Yoga releases what doesn't serve you and brings you back home to that which is true to you.

IN THE MIRROR

There's one other part of this unraveling business that's actually some fun, although surprising at times: to explore beyond the deeply internal mind-body healing work described above. After traveling the intentional grief path toward healing for some time, Annie began noticing what she noticed and realized that she didn't recognize the physical life she was living in as hers any longer. *My hairstyle didn't feel like me anymore. My wardrobe looked and felt like I was wearing someone else's clothes. Even the physical space of my home felt unfamiliar to me as though I was living in a space someone else had arranged, painted, decorated, and made their own,* Annie told me. She had arrived at a place so many of us before her have been where her inner landscape had shifted so drastically while becoming so much more deeply attuned to her needs. Her outer world no longer matched who she had become on the inside.

Many, like Annie, will hesitate even here. It took several months of working together before she was even willing to admit this dilemma about her physical world out loud to me. *I feel ridiculous,* Annie said. *It's like I'm having a mid-life crisis and I'm only 33 years old. If I start changing everything, people will really believe I've gone crazy. How much more stereotypical can I get than changing my hair and getting a tattoo after a year of being a widow. Shouldn't I just leave things the way they always were? I feel like wanting to change everything is just me being bored and irrational in my grief.* Just as most of us dishonor the changes many make at the "mid-life" mark in life, it seems to be status quo that grief makes us irrational when it comes to knowing what's best for ourselves too.

Once again, you find yourself noticing what you notice, getting curious about what you'd like to choose, and claiming permission you've always had to express yourself in ways that feel true to you. When you're coming to these decisions from within the nurtured, fully present space provided by the chrysalis, who can know better than you what is a true expression of who you're becoming? Annie went through a period of time where she reported she felt a bit like a teenager again, trying a few new looks before she found one that really suited her. She painted every wall in her house and moved some furniture a time or two before landing on a better flow and feel in her home, and even bought some new pieces too. Being intentional about curating an exterior to match the profoundly shifting inner world is a deeply inspired act of healing. Nothing makes it easier to commune with the authentic inner landscape of all that is you than feeling at home in the skin and house you're in. Be responsible and realistic with your working budget. Run your vision by a few of your closest and most trusted friends (whose opinion you value deeply) just for a sanity check. And remember, hair always grows back and you can always change your mind about that orange wall.

REFLECTION

Bodywork helps us heal because it allows our embodied traumas to move through while informing our thoughts and decisions too. Without tending to the healing of our body, it is significantly more difficult to fully commit ourselves to matters of the head and heart. Which bodywork practices or treatments feel accessible enough to try? What type of relief have you experienced in the form of truly compassionate hugs or professional healing work? Free write what feels most true for you right now as you complete the prompts below:

- *I feel most relaxed in my body when I…*
- *I feel most powerful in my body when…*
- *When I'm sad or upset, I notice my body feels…*
- *When something feels very true or safe to choose, I notice my body feels…*
- *I believe the mind-body connection is most relevant to…*

Chapter Ten

Reclamation

I first spoke to Lydia a few years after the death of her beloved Ray. I began our call by asking her to share her story of life after loss thus far with me so I could understand her unique experience with grief and what support she might be looking for. She shared some of the details surrounding her late husband's death and then got quiet for a moment before she started to tell me about the suffering she was experiencing in her life after loss.

I don't know how to move on, Lydia told me. *I just can't seem to pull myself together.* She told me about how she was able to function and was trying her best to be OK. Lydia was living alone, taking care of her home, and going to work every day. On the outside, she told me, everyone thinks I'm doing perfectly OK. She told me she still spent time with friends occasionally and she was working out a little like she was supposed to do to feel better. In the next breath, she was telling me while quietly crying that she was also having breakdowns at work that felt like they came out of nowhere. *I can't control when the crying starts, it just comes and it makes everyone around me so uncomfortable.* She told me she felt like she was disappointing everyone for still feeling so sad.

Lydia went on to share with me that no matter what she did, she just couldn't beat the feeling of emptiness. *I don't even feel like myself anymore*, she told me on that first call together. She talked about how tired she was; about how strong she has had to be and she just didn't feel like she had it in her to be strong anymore. Everything felt hard. *I have to do something*, Lydia said. *I don't want to live like this, but I'm not sure I believe it's possible to feel better.* She went on to tell me that she was afraid to feel better one day, that if that happened she would lose her connection to him. She told me that nothing felt like the right decision because she was getting conflicting advice and more judgment than she could handle from those around her. She felt like she never knew what to do.

During our work together, Lydia and I tenderly and methodically examined her grief journey, looking for signs of suffering and moving toward it with intention. We looked at her day-to-day life and she gradually created spaciousness in her schedule to slow down enough to truly feel and express her pain within the chrysalis she was slowly building. From that place, she also began establishing boundaries in several relationships where she was not feeling safely supported in her grief journey. We spent many a conversation looking at her fears and limiting beliefs, all thoughts that were controlling her life after loss. She was confusing thoughts with reality and feeling trapped until we worked through the reality of what was happening and she could understand that she was stuck in the in-between of grief, completely unraveled yet not yet in metamorphosis because she was trying with all her might to resist unbecoming the woman who had been married to her late husband.

In cultivating empowerment to trust the process and release that resistance, she began the practice of noticing what she noticed. Learning to notice when she felt pain and what she needed without filtering any of it changed everything for her. Lydia gradually learned how to cultivate a deeper awareness of how her late husband was still showing up in her life. No matter how mysterious or metaphysical it seemed, she never doubted the connection she now felt which allowed her to safely move forward into her life after loss without fear of losing him further. She also developed a simple ritual that she went to when she longed to feel a connection to him, a simple letter writing exercise she did in a journal dedicated only to letters written to him. *I just notice when I wish I could tell him something and I go write it down. It's fascinating how just the simple act of writing him a letter lifts the pain right away. I know he's not actually getting the letters but I can do something with my longing to communicate and that changes everything.*

In noticing what she noticed, Lydia started getting regular bodywork treatments from a holistic massage therapist in her town to support her chronic body aches and pains that didn't seem to go away, not even with pain medicines. She also started a gentle yoga practice and paid attention to keeping an earlier bedtime. She called me one week just giddy with delight about how good she was feeling in her physical body. She just couldn't believe what a difference a few weeks' worth of treatments had made. *Feeling so much lighter and more comfortable in my body is just giving me so much energy. I had no idea how exhausting it was to be in constant discomfort and pain.*

With her newfound energy, Lydia told me the "grief brain" fog that had been lingering for several years was lifting enough that she finally felt like she could really look at his death and her grief with new eyes. She was leaning in to the powerful thought work we were doing together that was helping her identify painful or limiting beliefs as just that: thoughts. *It's amazing how much this changes my experience,* she told me. *I always thought it was a little silly—people talking about mastering their thoughts. But when you and I talk about some of these things that have been so painful for so long, it's almost humorous now how incapacitated I felt by a belief. It felt so true until I could simply see it was something I could flip around and un-choose.*

After just a few months of working together, Lydia shared with me that she felt like she was finally coming home to herself. She told me that she felt like she was no longer just surviving her days, laughing that she felt like she was actually alive again. She also told me that she could see how everything was actually different in her life after loss because of his death and she was noticing for the first time how that didn't have to feel so scary. *It's actually pretty exciting,* Lydia told me. *I am learning who I am, maybe for the very first time in my life because of the work we're doing together. I'm learning how to make decisions about what I want for the first time in my adult life. I can't believe that it doesn't feel scarier. When I do feel anxious now, I know exactly what to do because of what we've talked about. I have no idea what my life after loss will become, but for the first time since he died, I'm excited to find out what that story will look like for me.*

This is my wish for you. I hope you too can end the cycle of suffering so you can stop surviving and thrive in life after loss. There is no greater gift to yourself than reclaiming the story of your life. The rest of your story is yours and it's waiting.

REFLECTION

Throughout this book, you've seen a wide-angle view of the journey through grief. Noticing what you notice, and keeping what feels true for where you are today on your journey, what is it you feel more ready to release with ease? What about your life do you feel inspired to take steps to reclaim? Take a quiet moment with a pen and paper to write freely.

- *I am aware of my grief most when…*
- *What I wish most for in my life after loss is…*
- *I would like to stop feeling…*
- *I am ready to do what it takes to…*

On Grief

A Manifesto

I f you find yourself ready to commit to intentional grief and reclaim your life after loss, this manifesto is for you:

I want to live in a world where grief is allowed to co-exist with living. Where sad is both safe and permissible, and yet, never requisite. Where joy is welcomed in guilt-free, sans judgment, and always accepted as true. I want to live in a world where the realm of possibility isn't restricted to happy OR sad, but seen instead for what it truly is: vast and endlessly shifting. I want to live in a world where people understand that the depth of our humanness allows us to feel heartbreaking devastation and pure joy too, one no more "real" than the other. I want to live in a world where "authentic" is the new little black dress: always appropriate and looks good on everyone every time.

I believe life after loss gives us a rich perspective on living, loving, and gratitude that few can truly access without a journey into grief. I believe because of who is missing from my life, I am able to more deeply appreciate those I have by my side. I believe it's safe to feel the pain and cry out with the guttural ache when it comes. I believe it's beautiful to welcome the giddiness of laughter, dance and inspiration that springs from the soaring heights when the time is right. I believe in allowing the authentic, true-for-you emotional experience to unfold and be expressed in ways that cultivate healing and integration.

I love finding ways to honor my late husband and incorporating his memory into our life in a way that feels safe and valuable to me. I love finding ways to honor who *I'm* becoming and incorporating joy, just for me, into this life where it feels right.

Here's what I know for sure: grief can make you feel invisible. To others, at first, and eventually to even yourself if you abandon what's true for you. There is no healing in disconnect; this is the place of forever pain so many believe is inherent to grief. Here's what I know for sure: grief is an intense journey we move through and the revelations, even more than the loss, will change our lives in powerful ways.

I am deeply committed to choosing what feels right and passing on what doesn't fit right now. I am committed to asking for what I need and letting go of what I don't. I am committed to changing my mind without making myself wrong for it. I am committed to self-care and room to breathe in the in-betweens of life's to-dos. I am committed to sobbing and smiling at the same time if it is the genuine expression of my soul in that moment. I am committed to saying "yes" to events that enrich me, and "no" to any offer that doesn't feel like a gift. I am deeply committed to trusting that come what may, within my authentic experience, every last drip of me is worthy and so deeply loved. I am committed to giving up the need to perform, and release the need to live up to perceived expectations of me. Instead, I commit to living fully, authentically, out loud, and in the moment as it comes. I am deeply committed to hearing "I love you." When others aren't quite able to meet me where I am on my journey, I choose to believe they're doing their best. I am committed to sharing when it feels safe and holding back when that feels safer.

I remain open to seeing magic. I remain open to shedding tears. I remain open to the connections I choose and seek refuge when that is what I most need. I remain open to learning from my pain. I remain open to experiencing true joy. I remain open to experiencing longing. I remain open to practicing gratitude. I remain open to knowing that gratitude and longing are allowed to walk hand in hand. I trust that the depth of my pain is not a reflection of the way I honor him, my life is. I remain open to receiving what comes next on this journey of life, knowing what has been will always be part of my story, and therefore, me.

Go gently, my friends. Go tenderly. Go with compassion toward what's real. Go fiercely forward with the courage to be vulnerable enough to know what's true for you. It's all information. It's all medicine. It's all life and it's waiting for you.

Acknowledgments

Behind the pages of this book is the tribe of friends, family, and healers who have been a profound piece of my journey in life after loss. They have each made a vital contribution to the tidal wave of energy that has propped me up in the depths and propelled me ever forward on my own journey through grief.

A deep and humble thanks to my children Peter, Betsy, Curtis, and Isla for their flexibility, understanding, and willingness to celebrate the writing of this book they can't yet read. I am forever grateful to their daddy, my beloved late husband Reid, my first love story, for co-creating a beautiful chapter of life with me. These four are the most precious gifts you ever gave me. They continue to be my teachers in all things.

To my darling Brad, thank you for bringing yourself so wholly to my side from the start of our story. There is vibrance and joy in life only love can put there. Thank you for choosing and celebrating life together with eyes and hearts wide open, and for holding sacred the chapter of my story before you that is mine to love, too.

To my parents Dale and Dianne and my parents-in-law Dale and Mary Ann: thank you for your helping hands and endless energy. I deeply appreciate the way you show up to love on my babies and create space for me to stretch and grow. Thank you for your continued celebration and support for all things unfolding in this unexpected chapter of life.

Susan and Stephanie, my dearest soul sisters, I love you and treasure our tribe. You have held me with unwavering love from the inception of this grief journey. Your dedication to honoring the truth of my experience allowed me to cultivate the insight, intuition, and awareness required for the healing I write about. Without your eyes to truly see me in this shadow, I surely would have been lost. I am forever grateful for all the tender and powerful ways you remind me of my right to rise and helped me learn again to trust my wings.

To Linda and Liza, the two beloved souls whose life passions guided me ever so gently to a new path in life in 2008. You are pure love and have shown me the way to motherhood, but more importantly, to coming home to myself. Thank you for what you model and for the energy you bring to spreading your truth. You are changing the world. You forever changed mine.

To our military family, local community, and every friend and kind human spread far and wide: I thank you for your bottomless love, kindness, encouragement, and generosity. You have cared for our family with such powerfully felt love at every turn since our Reid died and we so deeply appreciate the connection and care you continue to extend to us. He would be proud of the way his family has continued to be cared for.

To my healers and teachers who are powerful and abundant, I thank you for the carefully directed energy and attention you've offered me along the path. Each of you has been an agent of deep healing, teaching, integration, and reclamation. The list is long and likely incomplete, as I encounter new teachers and healers at every turn: Jeffrey Shoaf, Chad Wyatt, Yoganand Michael Carroll, Jacci Gruninger, Kara Tiede-Kabir, Mindy Meiering, Christina Allen, Michele Lisenbury-Christiansen, Ann Sheppard, Jen Terhune, and Elizabeth DiAlto.

Ongoing gratitude for the courageous clients and the powerful women in the Grief Unveiled Advisory Tribe whose heartfelt stories of their own unique grief journeys provided depth and insight during the creation of this book. I bow deep to your willingness to share so much with me. Thank you for inviting me to walk beside you.

A heartfelt thank you to Angela Laura, Cynthia Kane, and the entire powerhouse of a team at Difference Press behind bringing this idea to life. Thank you for helping me make a difference and bring my message of hope to the world. Without you, I would still be *thinking about* writing a book.

To the Morgan James Publishing team: Special thanks to David Hancock, CEO & Founder for believing in me and my message. To my Author Relations Manager, Margo Toulouse, thanks for making the process seamless and easy. Many more thanks to everyone else, but especially Jim Howard, Bethany Marshall, and Nickcole Watkins.

To you my readers, thank you so much for your courage to show up with an open heart to explore this challenging topic. There is so much gratitude for every one of you so willing to choose powerful vulnerability in the name of healing. Each of you who sends me stories of healing and transformation as a result of our work together fuels the fire behind my message. Together, we will be the change.

About the Author

Sarah Nannen is a grief and life coach, and the author of *Grief Unveiled*. Based on her own experiences and those of her clients, she writes candidly about the intense shadowland of widowhood and grief's many layers. She is the founder of an online grief coaching program dedicated to shifting the negative paradigm surrounding grief toward one of hope and possibility. While honoring the painful terrain that must be navigated in grief with intention, she boldly challenges the limiting cultural mythology of widowhood in her work.

126 | Grief UNVEILED

Sarah's up and coming podcast *Grief Unveiled: An Inside Look at Widowhood* continues the exploration far beyond the scope of this book.

Sarah is a veteran and military widow who lives in central Illinois with her partner Brad and their four children. In her "spare time," you'll find her teaching yoga, training for triathlons, or traveling with her family.

Website: www.sarahnannen.com
Email: hello@sarahnannen.com
Facebook: www.facebook.com/griefunveiled

Thank You

Sending you a heartfelt hug for making it through to this point in the book. Maybe you're feeling intrigued, and a bit of anticipation, too. Maybe you think you're ready to begin this journey through grief with your newfound awareness, but you're not sure where to start. If that's you, consider this your invitation to continue the exploration. There is even more material I wanted to include that a single book just couldn't accommodate.

If your curiosity is piqued and you're wondering if the time is right to lean into this journey with my support, go to www. griefunveiled.com to learn more about the ways I'm working with young widows to help them end the cycle of suffering and stop surviving so they can thrive in their life after loss.

I wrote this book to connect with others who are grieving and change the conversation we're having in our culture about grief, loss, and living. I'd love to learn about your grief journey and what in this book felt important to you. Connect with me at **hello@griefunveiled.com**. I look forward to hearing from you.

Morgan James
Speakers Group

www.TheMorganJamesSpeakersGroup.com

We connect Morgan James published
authors with live and online events
and audiences who will benefit
from their expertise.

CPSIA information can be obtained
at www.ICGtesting.com
Printed in the USA
JSHW050148231221
21468JS00001B/132